Tale of a multifaceted life

Volume 4
Enice Toussaint

Éditions Nouveau Siècle

Éditions Nouveau Siècle

Nouveau Siècle Publishing

The publishing house *"Nouveau Siècle (ÉNS)"* offers sincere and personal works where freedom of expression comes above all else. In our time, despite all conflicts, we live in an increasingly unified world. This is largely due to telecommunications and a global economy without borders. This new form of reality facilitates exchanges between cultures and the conceptualization of a human identity finally in harmony with itself.

It is within such a vision of peace that this publishing house intends to promote its activities: publishing personal words, born of individual experience, seeking to bear witness to a world in transformation. To move forward in this new century, we must go ahead without fearing change, difference, being oneself, one's thoughts, and those of others. With such a philosophy, true words, even the simplest ones, can help nurture the renewal of our world.

Mission statement of *"Nouveau Siècle"*: Sharing thoughts and preserving memories…

Publisher: Nouveau Siècle Publishing ENS

Email: ediontinsens@gmail.com

Website: www.enspublishing.com

Project Manager:

Natatsha Casimir

Book Cover Design:

Natatsha, Elle-Camay C. Reason, and Max Casimir

Cover Page Graphics:

Elle-Camay C. Reason

Photography, Makeup:

Natatsha Casimir

Website Design:

Audio Publishing

© 2001, Nouveau Siècle Publishing and Enice Toussaint

© 2004, Nouveau Siècle Publishing and Enice Toussaint for the English translation

Copyright

Nouveau Siècle Publishing ENS and Enice Toussaint

All rights reserved

Nouveau Siècle Publishing

ISBN: 978-1-80702-324-9 Printed Book

ISBN: 978-1-80702-323-2 Digital Book

ISBN: 978-1-80702-325-6 Hardback Book

Legal Deposit – 3rd Quarter 2025

Copyright

National Library of Québec

National Library of Canada – Digital Book

Table of Contents

Foreword 10

Chapter 1 11
  An Obstacle Course 11

Chapter 2 12
  On Benny Street, Montreal West 12
    Part One 12
    Part Two 14

Chapter 3 17
  Saint-Urban Street in Montreal 17
    Part One 17

Chapter 4 20
  Lacordaire Street in Montréal-Nord 20
    Part One 23
    Part Two 26

Chapter 5 32
  For the Fifth Time, I Try to Escape Jacques 32
    Part One 32
    Part Two 36
    Part Three 43
    Part Four 44

Chapter 6 49
  Rue Saint-André in Plateau-Mont-Royal 49
    Part One 49
    Part Two 53

Part Three 57

Chapter 7 63
   Third Return to Haiti 63
      Part One..63
      Part Two..66
      Part Three 71
      Part Four..77
      Part Five 80

Chapter 8 82
   My Incredible Saga with My Double.................82
      Part One..82
      Part Two..89
      Part Three 91
      Part Four..98

Chapter 9 100
   Easter in Montreal 100
      Part One..100
      Part Two..101
      Part Three 102
      Part Four..103
      Part Five 103
      Part Six 104
      Part Seven 106
      Part Eight...108
      Part Nine 109

        Part Ten 112

Chapter 10 114

    Construction of the House in Haiti..114

        Part One...114

        Part Two 116

        Part Three 117

        Part Four 122

        Part Five 125

        Part Six 128

Chapter 11 134

    Betrayal 134

        Part One...134

        Part Two 140

        Part Three 143

        Part Four 146

        Part Five 150

        Part Six 153

Chapter 12 157

    Definitive Return to Montréal..157

        Part One...157

        Part Two 160

        Part Three 163

Chapter 13 176

    I Return to Montreal..176

        Part One...181

Chapter 14 184
   The Beginning of 2002 184
Chapter 15 187
     Part One...187
     Part Two...188
     Part Three...196
Chapter 16 199
   The Hair Salon, Beautiful Encounters 199
     Part One...199
     Part Two...200
     Part Three...201
     Part Four..204
Chapter 17 206
   A Breakup Letter..206
     Part One...206
Chapter 18 213
   Jacques' Return to Montreal 213

Foreword

This autobiographical account immerses us in the inner life of a woman marked by sensitivity, faith, solitude, and the wounds of the past. Through an intimate and chronological narration, punctuated with memories and reflections, the author reveals her daily life with moving authenticity: errands, travels, family relationships, and moments of literary creation become reflections of her emotional state.

Around her revolve essential figures Natasha, Jacques, Lionel, Irène, Robert, Patrick, Max, etc. evoked with tenderness or tension, depending on the circumstances. This life journal, halfway between testimony and personal quest, reveals a resilient woman, on a path toward healing and recognition.

Spirituality holds a central place: Mass, prayers, and religious celebrations provide a reassuring framework amid inner turmoil. But above all, it is the family bonds, the moments shared with her sister, her grandchildren, her brother, that bring light and respite.

The writing, spontaneous and sincere, sometimes hesitant yet always touching, reflects a fragmented memory, a mind oscillating between past and present. This book is a precious work, a feminine voice daring to speak what many live in silence: the complexity of existing, of loving, of believing, and of rebuilding oneself.

D. M

Chapter 1

An Obstacle Course

In the meantime, a series of obstacles began to disturb my peace. Jacques would not stop harassing me on the phone, asking to meet with me. Each time, I refused. My sister Irène received a lawyer's letter about the house on Boyer Street she had co-signed the mortgage for us. So it was to her that the bank sent the repayment demand. This news shook me deeply. The matter had to be resolved very quickly. In the end, she found a way to pay the arrears, and we put the house up for sale so that we could rid ourselves of this debt. I wished to find work, but I did not yet have the health or the strength it would require.

I began to suffer from anxiety again. I remember the date of June 10, 1997, when I told Jacques that my sister had received a formal notice from the bank, and that she had managed to repay the amount due to regain peace. I will never forget that moment. He promised me he would do everything he could to repay all the debts to my sister.

Once again, I believed him. I will return to this story later.

In the meantime, my daughter was not doing well at all. At eight months pregnant, she was bleeding. She went to the hospital for tests. The doctors were trying to find out what was wrong. I was afraid. Her legs and feet were swollen; her circulation was not functioning normally. In the end, the doctors recommended rest. I then had to go much more often to her home to take care of the house and of her daughter, Elle-Camay, while her husband was at work. All those trips were becoming very heavy for me.

She and I discussed the situation, and I decided not to remain a boarder at the convent any longer. That way, Jacques could no longer harass me on the phone. Still, with much regret, at the end of the month, I left the convent to go live with my daughter on Benny Street, near Sherbrooke Street, in N.D.G. (Notre-Dame-de-Grâce).

Chapter 2

On Benny Street, Montreal West

Part One

Living with My Daughter

The apartment on Benny Street was a large 4 ½ on the upper floor of a duplex. My daughter and her family were living upstairs while waiting to move down to the ground floor, in preparation for purchasing the house. The ground floor was not rented out, but we still had access to it. We could do our laundry in the basement. The apartment was well ventilated and full of light. I shared a room with little Elle-Camay, and we were comfortably settled. The ground floor was more spacious. It had a large bedroom on the first floor as well as a dining room, a living room, a large kitchen, and a bathroom. The basement was an integral part of the house. Altogether, the house had three bedrooms, an office, a bathroom, and the laundry room.

My son lived with his fiancée not far from my daughter's home, on Sherbrooke Street West, near Cavendish. We could walk to his place. This allowed the family to see each other more often. We also had access to a library close by, and the church was on Terrebonne Street, at the corner of Benny Street, about a ten-minute walk from us.

Everything was going well for us. In the evenings, Patrick would tell us amusing stories to make us laugh. The little one was happy that I was there with them. Our big dog, Sisley, was funny in his own way. Sometimes, he would run away from the house. Natatsha and I would call him, and he would pretend not to hear us. Eventually, someone would let us know where to pick him up. But one day, he left for good and never came back. The whole family missed him. He was a good dog.

For a while, I decided not to stay in touch with anyone except my close family. I needed to regain my peace. Every Sunday, we went to Saint Joseph's Oratory, and then we would relax at Beaver Lake.

One day, I had a discussion with my daughter about Max and his father, Tony. I shared with Natatsha my idea of arranging for Max to meet his biological father. I also wanted to do this for my own inner peace. My conscience would then be at rest. She thought it was a good idea. I also spoke about it with my adoptive mother, who gave me this advice: *"It's very good, your idea, but you must prepare yourself for the possibility that if either one refuses, you won't let it affect you."* She promised she would pray for me.

So, I immediately began the process. I started by talking to my son. He responded by saying: *"If I do it, it's for you, because I have too many bad memories of that man."* Since he was about to leave for New York with his fiancée, he suggested waiting until his return. My daughter gave me Tony's phone number.

Right away, when I called him, he agreed. He asked me to call him back to set up an appointment. Two weeks later, after my son returned, I phoned Tony to arrange a meeting in a restaurant. He gave me this surprising answer: *"My lawyer advised me not to go to the meeting, so I won't come."* I replied to him: *"Now you know that I can sleep peacefully, because God sees that I have done my duty."* And I immediately hung up.

From that moment on, I felt at peace with myself, and I didn't think about it anymore. Max, for his part, assured me that his father's refusal didn't bother him and that he had agreed to meet him only for my sake. I told him I was glad that he viewed the situation positively. Sister Berthe, my sister, and my daughter were happy to see that I was handling it well. That was, in fact, the end of that part of my life. In the meantime, I was very busy taking care of my daughter and her baby, Elle-Camay, at home. The only unbearable inconvenience was that I had to go down to the basement to do the laundry

Part Two

Natasha's Delivery

Around July 15, we moved into the lower part of the duplex. Doing the laundry now became easier for me. My granddaughter Elle-Camay and I had our bedrooms in the basement. Natatsha and her husband slept in the room upstairs. The previous occupant of the house had died on the premises. While cleaning my room before moving in, I had found a funeral wreath in the closet. Since we had settled into the downstairs apartment, I constantly felt a presence. At night, I had nightmares. Elle-Camay was a very calm child. When she cried during the night, since her mother could not take care of her, and her room was next to mine, I was the one who looked after her.

I spoke to Patrick about my nightmares and this presence in the house. He admitted to me that he felt the same thing. One night, while I was sleeping, I suddenly felt a presence, and someone climbed onto me; I fought with it and woke up sweating. I prayed to God. The next day, I burned incense in the room and throughout the house. Still, I remained a little fearful. There were still pieces of furniture in the house that had belonged to the woman. Natatsha and Patrick sold them at a yard sale.

I was struggling with extreme fatigue. One day, we went to church, and my daughter could no longer walk. She was still bleeding. We took her to Saint-Luc Hospital on Saint-Denis Street, because her doctor worked there. It was discovered that the baby's blood was mixing with the mother's. So they prepared her for a C-section three weeks before the baby's expected due date. He was born on July 28, 1997. He was very big. He weighed ten and a half pounds and measured twenty-one and a half inches. Since he was born prematurely, all he did was sleep and nurse from his mother.

Two days after our return home, the mother's milk was no longer sufficient. We gave the baby another milk, and two weeks later, we began adding cereals. He was always hungry. At the child's birth, Jacques came to the hospital. It had been a very long time since I had seen him. The meeting had no effect on me. I was too preoccupied with taking care of my family.

Natatsha named her son Mikaël Raphaël Patrick. He was in good health. When she came home from the hospital, however, Natatsha was unwell. Because she was anemic, she suffered from chills and weakness. Patrick and I did our best to take care of her and the two children. I had no time for rest. After a week, Natatsha's health improved. She was now caring for the baby, and I looked after the household.

At first, Jacques had taken the habit of calling very often at Natasha's house. I suggested to my daughter that she make him believe I was absent. One day, he announced to Natasha that he would come to visit, under the pretext of seeing his grandchildren. Another day, he invited me to dinner at a restaurant. He swore that since his accident, he had changed, that he was no longer the same man, and that he no longer saw life the same way. In short, the usual seductive words. I remained on my guard. I was careful not to fall into another of his traps. However, my constant state of fatigue did not make things easy.

One day, he told me of his intention to take me shopping for a dress and shoes. At first, I didn't like the idea. I promised him I would think about it. Then I told myself that, after all, I deserved them, so I accepted. He came to pick me up. I questioned him about how he had so much money. He told me he had landed a big contract. He insisted that I make love to him. I resisted. He maintained that he loved me. I explained to him that I wasn't ready and that my wounds were still open. He offered to go on a trip with me. I refused. I told him that I knew my daughter needed me. All these attentions, he had never shown me in the past. He was now trying to be kind, gentle, and generous toward me.

Patrick went to the notary for the purchase of the house. The notary informed him that he had discovered hidden fraud on the house and that Patrick was the one who had to repay it. Patrick refused, and his deposit was returned to him. The little family then went to live with Patrick's mother in Repentigny while waiting to buy another house. As for me, I stayed with my friend Laura while I searched for an apartment.

Chapter 3

Saint-Urban Street in Montreal

Part One

My Stay at My Friend Laura's in October 1997

When I arrived at Laura's, I was not in good shape. I was having anxiety attacks. My back hurt, my chest hurt. I did not feel well at all, and I hardly slept at night. Sometimes, the pain on my left side was so intense that I felt like opening myself up to find out what was causing me such suffering. My doctor kept repeating that aside from my herniated disc, there was nothing else. Yet, I still wasn't well. No one realized the extent of my suffering, except my doctor and me.

Jacques, for his part, kept calling me at my friend's place. One day, without warning, he took me to a motel. This time, I made love with him. But I felt guilty. I remember that once the act was over, he confessed that it had been his last attempt. If it had failed, he said, he would not have been able to live without me. But he would have started fighting again to win me back. Despite all those sweet words, I remained on the defensive I no longer trusted him.

I told him that I was looking for an apartment. He said he knew one of our friends, who owned buildings in Montreal North, had some units available. I called this friend, who advised me to speak with his caretaker, which I did. The caretaker showed me a 4 ½, and the very same day, I signed the lease. I was happy to finally have an apartment of my own.

Here is what I wrote in my journal:

September 23, 1997 Journal

It is 3 a.m., and I cannot sleep. I've been awake I don't know for how long. I am still at Laura's. I was looking for an apartment, and I found one, thanks to God. I thank Him for that.

I moved in over the weekend. It's not because I wasn't comfortable at my friend's place far from it. It's because for two years, I had been moving from one place to another, between family and friends. Now it is time to take charge of my life. Moreover, I want to be independent, and I have many things to do. Jacques wanted to come live with me. I made him understand that, for now, I did not want to live with anyone. I wanted to be alone in order to take care of myself and to write. That was important to me.

I'll stop here. It is one in the morning. I will go to bed now until tomorrow.

Continuation of My Journal

Present Moment

December 17, 2006

These days, I don't have much time to devote to writing. Since it's the holiday season, I am obliged to share my time with family, friends, my sports colleagues, and people who need me. I have to buy gifts and send out invitations for Christmas. Despite all that, I feel in great shape.

Christmas is a holiday I love. At Christmastime, I forget all my troubles. I could say that I didn't choose the right moment to finish the remaining five years I still have to write about. But one can never know when the right time comes to do something.

I try to adjust to the situation. I neglect the little things I enjoy and the people I love in order to write. I feel that my grandchildren expect a lot from me. Mikaël kept asking me when I was going to finish writing my book. I would reply: *"Soon."*

He and Elle-Camay want me to spend Christmas at their place. They don't like the idea of my spending Christmas Eve alone. I think I will go to their house. But at the same time, I want to stay by myself because I want to finish writing the story of my past before the year 2007. I don't know if God approves of this.

This afternoon, I must go to my granddaughter Elle-Camay's ballet performance at 4 p.m. at Concordia University on de Maisonneuve Street.

(End of Journal)

I continue my story

Jacques was not happy with the idea that he would not be living with me. For me, it was better that way, too. I gave him permission to come and see me.

WiTh all the problems I had gone through, I needed to recharge myself. I was still living with anxiety and felt very vulnerable and depressed. I informed my daughter and my son so that they could better understand my state. Sometimes, they would say to me: *"Mammy, we don't understand what's wrong with you! Tell us!"*

Honestly, I didn't understand myself at that time. I very rarely called my sister, and that saddened me a lot. I suffered greatly from the silence between her and me. I didn't talk about it to anyone.

As for Jacques, even though I warned him that he would not be living with me, he was always there, and he took up a lot of space. I felt smothered. He did everything so that I would ask him to come live with me. But I remained firm in my decision. On October 1, 1997, I went to live alone in an apartment in Montréal-Nord, on Lacordaire Street at the corner of Henri-Bourassa Street.

Chapter 4

Lacordaire Street in Montréal-Nord

Living Alone in an Apartment in Montréal-Nord

Since I had left some furniture at my son's place, Jacques offered to pick it up for me. He and Max brought it to the apartment. It consisted of a loveseat, A small television, an electric recliner, a small dining set with four chairs, and a secretary desk. Since I didn't have a bed, Jacques took me to buy a mattress with its base. He paid for them for me. I thanked him, simply. I finished setting up my apartment. It was on the second floor. There was a long staircase. I set up an office in one of the two rooms I had. I planned to retreat there to pray and meditate on occasion. But also to write a little, because for some time writing no longer seemed as easy to me.

One day, I went to visit my sister and my brother. She barely looked at me. I entered my brother's room and greeted him affectionately. On my way out, I left a letter on the table giving my sister my contact details. I had specified that I now lived alone. She hardly said a word. I understood her. It was painful and humiliating for me, but there was nothing I could do then. I was going through a phase of my life where no one could help me. For example, I no longer showed up for my appointments with my therapist. I felt lost.

I lived with my anxiety and my fears. Jacques came to my place every day. He even showed up twice on the same day at times. He harassed me by bringing up gossip invented by Tony, my ex-husband. He told his friends that he could still sleep with me if he wanted. He insisted that I call Tony, with whom I had not been in contact for a long time, to issue warnings that I found completely ridiculous. "Never I will not do you that honor!" I exclaimed. I kept telling him not to come back to my place, because I had had enough of all that. Day after day, he would return calmly to apologize.

At the same time, I had the impression that he was spying on me from afar. Under those circumstances, I never accepted that he sleep at my place. I often walked around the neighborhood. It had two shopping centers. I strolled there frequently by myself. I didn't buy anything, but it did me good to see something different and to meet other people.

Every Sunday, I walked to Saint-Colette Church. Not owning a car, I walked a lot. At Thanksgiving, Yole's family, my son's fiancée, had invited me to dinner at her home.

I accepted the offer with the intention of getting to know her better. I was very well received and had an excellent evening. Upon returning home, I did not feel well. My heart hurt. I was anxious again. Taking a sedative helped me fall asleep.

Natasha used to come and spend a day or two at my place with her children. I enjoyed her visits; I felt less lonely. I had fun with my grandchildren, especially with Elle-Camay. I sang and danced with her. I enjoyed those moments very much. I had noticed that I was happy with my grandchildren. Sometimes, Natasha would leave them with me to run errands. Since I didn't have much money, I lacked the funds to buy food. Jacques would pick me up every Friday to get food from the food banks. The process embarrassed me, but it was necessary. As for Jacques, he never went inside. He always waited for me in the car.

Back at my place, I shared the food with him. He brought his portion to his cousin's, where he lived. He had really dragged me down without me realizing it. He claimed he had no money. I believed him. I will return later to this story about money.

Despite everything, I did not fully trust him. Toward the end of October, after many refusals, I finally agreed to make love with him. That time, I let myself go a little. He was delighted. "Finally, you decided!" he exclaimed. I told him that there was no question of his staying the night at my place; he had to leave. He tried to change my mind, but in vain. There was an inner voice whispering to me not to lower my vigilance, not to trust him. He was not sincere, and he would want even more.

I Confide in My Journal

10 p.m. This afternoon, December 18, 2006, I went to the performance of my little Elle-Camay. She did very well. She was very radiant. The whole family was there. Afterwards, we went to have dinner in a nice restaurant. I had a good evening with my loved ones.

Today, while writing this morning, I had a small asthma attack; I felt the same stress as in the past.

I Continue My Story

One fine day, after I had made love with Jacques, he started grumbling that my furniture was badly arranged in the living room and that I should move the armchair. His comments awakened very bad memories in me. I immediately told him that no one could tell me what to do in my own home. Since I had agreed to make love with him, he already believed he had the right to dictate my behavior. I asserted myself clearly. I especially did not want him to walk all over me. He left without saying a word. He came back, harassing me again about his desire to spend the night at my place. We argued nonstop. He seemed upset when Natasha brought the children to my place. I let him talk. From then on, he came less often. I paid him no attention. I felt at peace when he didn't come.

The holidays arrived. At Christmas 1997, I welcomed my little family. The atmosphere was joyful and relaxed. It was at that moment that Yole and Max decided to get married. Jacques was among us.

That evening, he filmed everything. After dinner, he drove Yole and Max back to their place.

On New Year's Eve, I stayed alone because the children had been invited to their in-laws' homes. At midnight, I was sleeping peacefully in my bed. I had also been invited, but I wanted to be alone at home. I prayed and I meditated. I felt at peace with myself.

It is midnight, and I am going to bed.

Present Moment

Tuesday, December 19, 2006

It is 4 a.m. I have been awake since 3 a.m. I can't fall back asleep, so I decided to get up. I had a headache and chest pain. I must continue writing in order to finish my book. At the same time, I fear neglecting those I love during this Christmas season. I feel pulled in two directions, and it unsettles me a little.

When I woke up at 3 a.m., I made myself a parsley tea and read a Christmas story that a good friend had left me, titled *Juliette's Message*. Just yesterday evening, without having read the book, I was speaking of this very message to my daughter. I confided in her how happy I was to see Max and Patrick playing with their children something their father never did with her or her brother. I think many people don't realize it. Yet this behavior greatly helps children's development. Memories that follow them all their lives.

I Continue My Story.

Part One

Vivianne's Illness   December 1997

During the month of December, my adoptive sister, Vivianne, was admitted to the emergency room at Notre-Dame Hospital. She had contracted an infection. The doctors discovered she had suffered a heart attack. They performed a bypass. She remained in the hospital for two weeks. Then she returned home to recover. I visited her very often. It was a difficult trial for the family. She stayed home during the holiday season. Usually, on New Year's Day, she spent the day at my sister's. In fact, she would arrive on New Year's Eve and go back home on January 2. This time, she was alone at home. That night, I too was alone, and I called her, thinking her daughters were with her. She answered with a sad voice: "Happy New Year!" She then told me she was alone. "If I had known you were alone, I would have come to spend New Year's Eve with you," I told her. She replied that it would be for another time, and we hung up.

At that time, there was great coldness between my sister and me. I avoided going to her place too often. I would call her from time to time, but on her side, there was silence.

During the holidays, I went to see her. She welcomed me with an awkward silence. Even though Jacques didn't live with me, she didn't like the fact that I was seeing him. I respected her way of looking at things.

During January, my daughter experienced problems with her mother-in-law. She came to my place more often. Her husband, Patrick, was sick. Later on, she decided to come live with me alone with the children, while waiting for Patrick to buy a house. During her stay with me, I felt happy, but Jacques didn't appreciate her presence. He came to see me less often.

In the meantime, a friend, Hermine, sold me her husband's used car. I was very pleased with the deal, as I could then more easily meet my needs.

Since Jacques could no longer come and harass me at home because of my daughter's presence, he did it over the phone. He called me very often. Sometimes, he would call and then hang up without saying a word. When he came, he always put on a hypocritical face. I didn't let it bother me. One day, he asked me this question over the phone: "If the car insurance compensates me for my accident, what will you do with the money?" I answered that I would repay the debts we owed my sister. "Ah!" he said. And he hung up. I had the impression he was hiding something from me.

It was only months after that phone exchange that I learned he had already received a large sum of money and had been receiving payments every two weeks as compensation for his lost salary. During all that time, he claimed to be in need and took me to food banks to collect groceries, which I then shared with him. I could have left that food for people who really lacked it.

I stopped going to food banks when my friend Laura found out. She shouted at me: "Not you, Enice! I won't let you go beg for food!" She was a single mother. She made it a point to bring me a bag of groceries each week. And Jacques didn't react. But the worst part is that he would take some of it.

When I think of all these things, I feel outraged. My children couldn't help me; they had their own financial problems. And I didn't want to beg from anyone else. My sister Irène and our friends believed I was doing well, financially and morally, because, despite my problems, I was always well dressed and in a good mood. To everyone around me, I was leading a normal life and had no need of support.

Yet I remember that when I was little, my mother often repeated this advice: "Never let it be known if things are going badly at home, whether financially or morally. You must always be clean on the outside as well as on the inside." As she grew older, my sister Irène continued to give me this same advice. Even today, I've noticed that my daughter passes it on to her children.

During the short time I lived with my mother, I had the chance to learn many things by listening to her speak to my older brothers and sister. And I believe my sister continued this work with Sister Berthe. On that note, I sometimes find that Irène is very harsh toward me. One of her friends once confided this to me: "You know, Enice, if your sister speaks to you that way, it's because she loves you. To her, you and Robert are her children, and your children are her grandchildren."

Her remark instantly awakened something very powerful within me. I had the intuition of it, but my rebellious side didn't want to believe it. I was too hurt inside to accept it. I realized that the more I go back into my past, the more I change in my inner nature. That is why I am eager to reach the year 2003, which will mark the end of my autobiographical account.

Part Two

The Dramatic Death of Vivianne in March 1998

Before writing this part of my past, I lit a candle. I prayed and walked a little in the hallway of my apartment. It was in order to find the inspiration and courage to do it.

Life was going well. My grandchildren were very happy. From time to time, I would go walking at the mall with them and my daughter. Patrick came every day for a short visit.

Vivianne had gotten better. One day, she came to my place to have hair extensions put in by my daughter. She seemed to be in better health. When she left, Natasha told me she had something to confide and didn't want me to repeat it. She admitted she had the impression that Vivianne didn't have long to live. Her body was there, but she

was empty inside. I answered that we needed to pray for her.

On February 27, there was that ice storm which caused several power outages. But at my place, there was no loss of electricity. We were very happy about that. I thanked God especially since I was hosting the children at that time.

Jacques had called me to inform me that his electricity was cut and that he wanted to come sleep at my place. I accepted his request. On the evening of February 28, 1998, when he arrived, we were watching television in the living room. When it was time to sleep, Natasha, as usual, went to bed in the first bedroom with her little boy, while Elle-Camay and I went to the other bedroom. We slept with the bedroom doors left open. I had prepared the living room sofa for Jacques. But he insisted on sleeping with me in my bedroom, in my bed.

I told him it was impossible. I firmly explained that I was willing to help him, but I would not tolerate him trying to dictate my conduct in my own home.

He objected, saying that if I didn't let him sleep in my bedroom and in my bed, he would leave the next morning, and I would never see him again.

"Do as you wish!" I retorted. The next day, he indeed left. For a while, I had no news from him. I didn't worry, being occupied with my daughter and her children.

During the week of the ice storm, Vivianne had a small misunderstanding with her two daughters. The eldest went to live with a neighbor for a while until the situation calmed down. Vivianne's older sister, Fabienne, who lived in Haiti, called to ask about her health and to check whether the ice storm had caused them much damage. Vivianne replied that her health had improved, but that, for a time, her eldest daughter had gone to stay with a neighbor. In reality, Vivianne had not fully recovered. She was still in convalescence, slowly getting back up, but she remained fragile.

The next afternoon, a family member from Haiti called to inform Vivianne that her older sister Fabienne had died earlier that day. Vivianne was in shock. She shared the news with us. We were stunned by Fabienne's sudden death. At the same time, my sister, close friends, and I went to her place to offer her advice and support.

Vivianne was clearly not healthy enough to travel. So three days later, my sister Irène and Vivianne's eldest daughter, Marlène, left for Haiti to attend the funeral. Just before their departure, Vivianne suffered another attack. She was admitted to the hospital. During her stay, I went every day from 9 a.m. to 8 p.m. to keep her company.

When my sister left for Haiti, I had promised her that I would take care of Vivianne. Given her condition and the deep grief that overwhelmed her, there was no question of leaving her alone. The doctors decided to perform another bypass to unblock an artery. On the eve of the operation, one of our friends, Marie, washed Vivianne's hair. That day, several people came to visit her. A doctor entered the room and gave me this warning:

"Madam, we are going to take a chance to unblock the arteries, but you know, they have become as small as spider threads. You must pray."

My sister and Marlène had left for a one-week stay in Haiti. Their return was scheduled for Saturday. Vivianne's operation was planned for the same Saturday. It went well. That day, I did not stay very late at the hospital. My plan was to return early Sunday morning to take Vivianne to Mass at the hospital chapel.

The next morning, Sunday, I had arranged to meet Irène so we could go together to the hospital. Entering Vivianne's room, I made no comment to my sister. Yet I immediately felt that her eyes looked like those of a person about to pass away. Her face was fresh and radiant, but it was not natural.

We kissed her. Irène was crying. We went to Mass. All three of us could not stop crying, especially my sister. After the service, the priest and a few parishioners came to speak with us. We told them about Vivianne's illness and the circumstances of her sister's death.

Back in her room, she suggested that we go to the waiting room, as we would be more comfortable there to talk. She then turned directly to my sister: *"I want you to tell me everything about the funeral, from beginning to end."* Once we were settled comfortably, my sister recounted everything in detail. I asked her how the deceased had been dressed and styled. Her description was very precise: *"Fabienne was wearing a white dress with pale blue stripes. Her hair was braided into two plaits."* I sat there in thought. My sister wanted to know what was on my mind. I complied with her request: *"Last night, I saw Fabienne in a dream she was dressed exactly that way."* They both seemed very surprised by my dream.

Since it was time for dinner, we returned to the room. Her meal tray had already arrived. We helped her into an armchair and placed the table in front of her. She refused to eat. My sister urged her to take a few bites. Her dream was that after her illness, I would travel to Haiti with her for a few days. Irène and I encouraged her to find strength again. She was extremely sad. It was a very difficult moment for the three of us.

I could not confess to Irène the feeling I was experiencing. I was afraid of hurting her. I sensed the imminent death of Vivianne. It was a very powerful feeling. We placed her in her bed, surrounding her with several pillows. Irène raised the head of the bed very high. She was then more comfortable. My sister Claire from Haiti had sent her a Bible and an image of the Virgin. Irène placed them in her hands. She held them and curled up in her bed like a little child with her doll. She placed them between her stomach and her heart. It was painfully sad to see her. We whispered to her: "Bye, bye, bye, Vivianne." She responded with a smile. I then assumed that she was acting like a little child gathering her toys before leaving.

We met a friend at the elevator door who was going to visit her. We recommended that she not stay long because Vivianne seemed tired and needed to sleep. She offered to wait for us. She went up and came back very quickly. She told us that she had greeted her and that she would return with us a little later.

To return to Irène's place on Mentana Street, near Duluth Street, we crossed Lafontaine Park, which took only a few minutes. As soon as my sister opened the door, the telephone began to ring. Irène had just enough time to take off her boots and pick up the receiver. She was told to return immediately to the hospital because Vivianne had just passed away. Thus, while we were crossing the park, in about ten minutes, she was already gone.

It was unbearably painful. We called her daughters and returned there to see her one last time. When I touched her, she was still warm, but the middle of her head was cold. It was certainly the end. The two sisters had died within a span of fifteen days. Irène never recovered from these deaths, especially from that of Vivianne. To continue living, she had changed many things in her daily life and her behavior.

Her children and all her friends deeply mourned her. She loved life so much; she was full of humor and made us laugh to tears at our evening gatherings.

I cannot find the words to describe her. My daughter Natatsha she had gone to do her hair and makeup in her coffin. Her daughter, Milly had accompanied Natasha. During the preparations for the funeral, I had been entrusted with her small suitcase, which contained her important documents and her jewelry, so that I could keep them safe.

One morning, I sat down in my living room and touched the little suitcase with a great sense of respect. Before opening it, I spoke to Vivianne: "Forgive me, I am going to enter your intimacy. Help me to do it, I need you." I was very moved as I opened the suitcase. She had placed one of her photos inside the cover. It was as if she were there. I felt her presence.

She is a woman I will never forget. She suffered greatly in her childhood and in her adult life.

A Little Reflection

In recounting my past, I think of her, of my friend Josie, and of all the other women who suffer in silence, who do not dare to speak about it, or who are afraid to do so. Or even those who died without ever taking the time to break free.

Chapter 5

For the Fifth Time, I Try to Escape Jacques

Part One

I Leave the Apartment in Montréal-Nord

March 1998

After Vivianne's death, I told Natatsha that I would not stay in the apartment. She, too, no longer wanted to live there. I had not heard from Jacques for two weeks. When he called, he wouldn't speak. I no longer wanted to answer the phone because I felt it was being tapped.

In the meantime, Natatsha and Patrick had found a house in Ahuntsic, in the west of Montreal, a duplex. The house was in very poor condition. The painting had to be done, the floor repaired, etc. I told Natasha that we had to move as quickly as possible, without telling Jacques. I would leave behind the desk and the belongings he had lent me; I would hand the apartment key over to the caretaker. I notified the landlord, and a week later, I left the apartment. On the last trip of the move, a police officer came knocking at the door. He couldn't tell us the reason for his visit. I felt Jacques's presence nearby. To frighten us, he was capable of anything. I had asked my sister Irène if she could take us in for a few days while Natasha finished painting her house. She agreed.

Her home had a very large bedroom. She, the children, and I all slept in the big room. It had a large bed, a small bed, and a crib. Natatsha slept in another room on a small bed because every morning she left early to work at the new house and came home late at night.

Mikaël, the baby, was 8 months old. He was a sturdy baby, very heavy. When he woke up at night, he literally screamed. My sister and I would both wake up like two frantic women. I would change his diaper while Irène prepared the bottle. One night, he fell off the bed while I turned my head to grab a wet cloth. He was already lying on the floor. He wasn't hurt. Since birth, he had been so heavy that we could not carry him in our arms for long.

One day, Jacques called my sister's house. She answered the phone. He asked to speak to me. I really don't know how he found out I was staying at Irène's. That day, he found out who he was dealing with, because my sister told him he had no right to call her home. They argued.

From then on, we never heard from him again. We stayed only a week at Irène's because she had to go back to work the following week. We didn't want her to get too tired. Since Natasha and Patrick's house wasn't quite ready, the week after that, we went to stay with my son. Because of the smell of fresh paint, the children couldn't stay in the house yet.

At Max's, everything was fine. My daughter-in-law, Yole, helped me a lot. The apartment was spacious, and Max gave us a very large bedroom. We were finally able to set up the two cribs and my bed there.

After a week, Natasha and her family moved into their house in Ahuntsic on Clarke Street, not far from Crémazie, and I stayed at my son's for a while, waiting to find an apartment. I was starting to get tired of all this coming and going, of living out of my suitcase, and I needed rest. I also needed to have a clear head before calling my lawyer. I planned to talk to him about the separation process.

A few days later, I did call him. I told him that I was no longer with Jacques and that I wanted to meet with him regarding the separation or divorce process. When I arrived at his office, he seemed surprised to note that I had resumed the divorce proceedings and not the separation. I wanted to obtain information regarding Jacques' car insurance policy and the compensation terms after his accident. He asked me a few questions about this and promised he would get back to me soon.

In the meantime, I continued my quiet little life at my son's. The house was calm. I could rest without being disturbed.

We had reached the beginning of April 1998. I learned that Jacques had a girlfriend; it was the same woman who lived in Toronto. His action didn't surprise me because my intuition had already made me suspect it. That same day, in the afternoon, my lawyer informed me that Jacques was receiving money every two weeks from the automobile insurance company. But he had declared that he would not pay me alimony. This news, too, I had anticipated; I expected the answer about alimony would be negative. I remember saying to the lawyer: "Leave it, I don't want his money." Deep inside, I wished Jacques good luck with that money.

But the lawyer pointed out that the case was not closed. He was conducting research to verify if Jacques had received compensation money, because if that were the case, he would have to share it with me. I responded with these words: "You know, do what you want. For now, I must focus on my health and on myself."

It was April 7, 1998. After learning all this news, I felt anxious. I took an Activant pill before going to bed, and I prayed. I asked God to send me my guardian angel and to give me the joy of love and peace in my soul so I could have a good night. It didn't take long. I quickly fell asleep. I dreamed. I saw that a man who looked like the unknown friend was rocking me. He was very affectionate toward me, and I felt very happy. I tasted a peace I cannot describe. When I woke up, I was filled with a faith that nothing could take away. From that day on, I became stronger. I wanted to push forward and become myself again, but my health was still fragile.

It was early April. It was Lent. On the eve of Good Friday, I went to sleep at my sister's. I knew it was a difficult time for her because every year, Vivianne used to come sleep at her house in order to attend the March of Forgiveness that took place in the streets of Montreal. The faithful would leave at 7 a.m. from the east of Montreal, from Henri-Bourassa Boulevard at Sainte-Madeleine-Sophie Church, to finish their march at Notre-Dame Church downtown at 3 p.m. Along the way, they would stop at 14 churches to pray.

For Irène, the course of things had become depressing because Vivianne constantly accompanied her. If I decided to go to her place, it was mainly to encourage her. My persistent back problems prevented me from walking too long.

That morning, after she left, I went to Natasha's. I helped her a little with the children. At 3 p.m., we went with the kids to attend the Good Friday ceremony at the nearby church. After kissing Christ, little Elle-Camay was overjoyed. Over the days, with my comings and goings between my daughter's, my sister's, and my son's, I was constantly living out of my suitcase. I no longer had a home of my own; I had become almost a wanderer.

The whole family was ready to help me. My son would take me to restaurants and to the movies with his wife. Our friend Dédé took Irène and me to Trois-Rivières and Sainte-Anne-de-Beaupré. I often went out with my daughter and her children. But deep inside, I felt the need to be at home, among my things. So, I decided to start looking for an apartment in a neighborhood close to my son's. The apartments in that area were almost new. The only thing left was for me to make a decision. But at the same time, I was troubled. I couldn't settle on a choice. Should I go live in another province for a year or rent an apartment? Then I would finally stabilize and stop moving around. I was discouraged by this situation, by moving from house to house. Moreover, it was time for me to start writing again. I realized that every time I found a bit of peace and started writing again, something always happened, and some obstacle arose to stop me.

Since my son was to be married on June 13, I made the decision to move after the wedding.

In the meantime, wedding preparations had begun. It was to take place in two months, and much remained to be done. Max and Yole decided to design their wedding invitations themselves.

Part Two

My Journal

I want to insert here a few passages from my journal to show how my life was unfolding at that time.

April 17, 1998   Journal

My daughter called me to ask if I could take her to the clinic with her Mikaël. I spent the whole day with them. Mikaël had bronchitis. Around 3:30 p.m., I went to pick up Irène to take her to the Winners store. Then I came back home.

April 18, 1998   Journal

Max and Yolanda went out to do their groceries. I'm waiting for them to come back so we can go out, because I lent them the car. In the meantime, I'm reading a few parts of my journal.

I just read a page I wrote on July 8, 1996. I felt chills. I was describing the way Jacques treated me in Haiti. My heart ached because I had declared that I would never go back to him, unless it was God's will. Yet, I let myself be taken aback four more times. My God, I never want to go back to that man again. I feel so good when I'm not with him. I never thought I would feel so much hatred for him. Let him go to hell!

When Max and Yolanda came back, I went to Irène's and then to my daughter's, because she wanted to take part in a young entrepreneurs' contest. We talked about everything and nothing. We had fun with the children. I was happy.

I went back to Irène's because she had invited me to spend the weekend at her place. I arrived around 9:15 p.m. Our nephew Riva was there. It had been a long time since we had seen each other. We talked about many subjects. One of my sister's friends came to visit her. We spoke about Jacques, my sister's tenant who lives upstairs and who has become her friend. He invited us over for dessert and a few glasses of wine. We danced. That relaxation did me good because it had been so long since I had danced. I had a good evening and also a good day. I thanked God.

Sunday, April 18, 1998 Journal

When I woke up this morning, Irène was already dressed to attend the 7 o'clock mass at Saint Jude Church. I hurried to get ready as well. I wanted to go to mass. When we returned home at 8:30, Marcel and Claude, family friends, called to let us know they would come pick us up at 9:30 for a mass in honor of the late Viviane at Notre-Dame de Lourdes Church on Sainte-Catherine Street, at the corner of Berri.

After mass, they invited us for breakfast at their home on Papineau Street, across from Lafontaine Park. We ate well and drank wine. It was a good morning.

After returning to my sister's, since it was the feast of Saint Denis, patron of the church on Laurier Street, at the corner of Berri, we went to attend the ceremony held at 4 p.m. in honor of the Saint. We walked there.

Back home, we were exhausted. It was dinnertime. Our friend Dédé came to visit my sister, and she invited him to have dinner with us. After dinner, I left. Despite my fatigue, I was happy to have spent a good weekend of rest and prayer. Today, April 19, is Jacques' birthday. I didn't call him. I will not give him the honor of a call. I haven't spoken to him since February 27, 1998. It's late, I'm going to bed. But first, I will thank God for my day.

Present Moment

Today, December 26, 2006, I am at my daughter's in Saint-Constant. I am settled in my granddaughter's room. I had come to spend Christmas with the little family. Mikaël and his sister Elle-Camay had been asking me for a month. They kept telling me they didn't want me to spend Christmas alone. I've been here since December 24. Before Christmas, I hadn't written anything since Wednesday, December 20. I wanted to share the joy and magic of Christmas with my children and grandchildren, my sister, my brother, and my dear friends.

On Thursday, I used the day to finish my Christmas shopping. On Friday, with my granddaughter and grandson, I prepared two trays of gingerbread cookies and sugar cookies. Then, small meat and tuna pies. Usually, I used to make them to give as gifts to family and close friends, but for years, I had stopped making them. This year, I was motivated by my grandchildren. Also, I feel better inside. When my brother Robert tasted the cookies and pies, he said to me, *"You haven't lost your touch, even if it's been a long time since you baked."*

On Saturday, December 23, our friend Dédé had invited my sister and me to a restaurant. We didn't go far from Irène's place. It was on Rachel Street, a French restaurant (Les Infidèles) near Saint-Hubert Street. It was a very pleasant evening. I stayed the night at my sister's. I wanted to spend time with her and my brother Robert. My day with them was excellent. The next day, Sunday, I took Irène to do her last-minute Christmas shopping at Bernard Flowers on Bernard Street. She bought several beautiful bouquets. With me, she went to deliver the flowers: to my daughter at her hair salon, to Sister Berthe, our adoptive mother, and to one of her friends. When we got back to her house, it was around 3 p.m. I only stayed for a short while. I left around 4:30 p.m. for Saint-Constant, to my daughter's.

I had a good Christmas at Natatsha's. On Christmas Eve, we went to midnight mass at Saint-Constant Church. When we returned, we had a meal and unwrapped the gifts. The next day, December 25, my son came with his wife and children. They too unwrapped their gifts. The children had a great time. So did we.

I felt so happy to be with my little family. Thinking about everything happening in the world, I was radiant and I thanked God for His goodness. I'm going back home at noon today. It's snowing. This is the first snowfall of the winter, and the temperature is mild.

April 28, 1998   Journal

Today, I went to therapy. I cried a lot, proof that I still have many things inside me that I don't know how to get rid of.

The days go by, and my life feels like a labyrinth. I hadn't stopped with all the comings and goings. I was always carrying a bag from house to house. I thought of myself as crazy and even told my sister so, and anxiety was overwhelming me.

One thing that helped me was the preparation for my son Max's wedding. Since they were already living together, it was up to them to prepare their wedding and get help from the family. On my side, I couldn't do much because I had no money.

As for Jacques, we didn't count on him. So, my sister offered to help us by taking full responsibility for the reception. For that, I had to contribute manually and morally. For a few weeks, I didn't write in my journal. I resumed writing on Mother's Day evening.

May 10, 1998   Journal

Today is Mother's Day. I went to an Anglican church with my son and his fiancée. I attended a beautiful ceremony. When we returned home, I took a nap. I woke up at 3:30 p.m. It did me good. I felt calmer and more relaxed. When I woke up, I called my sister.

Then, Max, Yole, and I went to Yole's family's house for dinner. At dinner, the subject of conversation was centered on the wedding. I had a good Mother's Day. We came back around 8:00 p.m. It was drizzling, and the weather was damp. So, I settled down a little more relaxed to watch television. Thanks to Jesus for this good day. End of journal.

I continue my story

In the meantime, I had to find a way to give a gift to my son for his wedding. One of my cousins, Jojo, told me about a job that could earn me a little money in Île Bizard. I was supposed to replace a woman for two days. I went there. I couldn't stay for the two days. It was too difficult for me, especially with my back problem. I had to take care of eight people. I had to prepare their food, wash them, and put them to bed for only 40 dollars, and I was alone with them in a big house. I was a little scared. Above all, I didn't know there was so much work.

When my son found out why I went there, he was not happy. He told me: "Mamy, I don't need a gift, your presence will be my gift. You are here, with your love and your warmth, that is all I need from you." I was reassured, but still, with the 40 dollars, I bought him a small portable vacuum cleaner as a keepsake. Yet, I had called Jacques to tell him about his son's wedding. Max had sent him an invitation card. He did not give any sign of life. Even though he had received the car insurance money. I didn't know the amount. He didn't give a cent for the wedding.

Through my lawyer, I learned that Jacques had received a sum of money. He had promised me that he would pay off the debts to my sister and to other people. But instead of that, he went to Haiti, leaving me a letter saying that he had left me the land that was in Haiti and that I should give him 2000 dollars when I sold it. He let me know that he didn't have to give any money for the wedding. Yet we hadn't asked him for anything. I didn't answer him. I didn't want to stress myself with that. As for the land, I had already sold a part of it for hospital expenses.

In the meantime, I didn't worry about those problems with him. The only thing I had to do was to keep trust and have faith.

Here are some pages from my journal.

May 27, 1998 journal

I just remembered that I lost everything. My furniture and all my personal belongings stayed in Haiti. I lost all my jewelry, my health. All of that because of one person, Jacobi, but I still have my dignity.

I was just refused another apartment, all because of him. I have too many debts. I cried. My sweet Jesus, I need a place to live. Help me find an apartment so I can have my own place. You know, Jesus, I can't take it anymore. I don't know if this time I can take it positively, it's stronger than me, I can't think about it anymore.

I called my sister to ask her to phone about renting in the apartment blocks on Saint-André Street, just steps away from her home. "I forgot to mention that after yesterday's news, I prayed to God so I would stay positive all the time and that the bad news wouldn't affect me. So, last night, while praying, I asked God to make me forget this bad day and let me have a good night. I slept the whole night without taking anything."

When she came back, my sister called me to tell me that instead of just taking the number, she did better than that. She went straight to the office, and there was only one apartment left. She told me she made an appointment in an hour. I had to hurry to get there.

She came with me to the appointment. When we arrived, the manager showed us the apartment. It was a 2 ½ with one closed bedroom, and I liked it. We went back to the rental office. She asked me for an ID card, and my sister told her she would co-sign for the apartment, so she also presented her card.

She had us sign the lease right then and there. It was like a miracle. The day before, I had been refused, and the next day I had my apartment. All thanks to my sister and thanks to God. You must never get discouraged. You just need to have faith. I was very happy. I think it is precious. I am supposed to move into the apartment on July 1th.

May 30, 1998 journal

I have been awake since 4 a.m. I can't sleep. There are too many things in my head. My apartment, Max's wedding, Natasha, who has so many things to do, and I must help her. There was also my sister, whom I should help with Max's wedding.

Yesterday, May 29, I went with my sister and my brother Robert to buy his suit for the wedding. Everything went well. He chose beautiful, good-quality clothes and comfortable shoes.

Today, I had a big day. I wanted to go give a hand to Natasha, who was having a garage sale. My sister took Yolanda and her mother for the flowers, and I also had a meeting at 7 p.m. Anyway, I'll just let time take care of things.

I am not stressing myself. It is 7 a.m., and I just finished my morning prayer. I feel ready to start my big day.

Finally, around 9:30 a.m., Jacobi, Irène's tenant, who is supposed to prepare the reception in her backyard, called Max and Yolanda to come to choose the flowers. My daughter canceled her garage sale.

The meeting was canceled, too. In the end, I only took part in Jacobi's and my sister's garage sale. Around 1 p.m., I came back home for a quiet evening. End of journal.

Part Three

Preparations for Max's wedding

Max's wedding was to take place in 13 days. There were still many things left to prepare. Among other things, I had not yet bought my dress. I had decided to dress in gold. It took me a whole day of shopping to find what I was looking for: a dress and gold shoes.

My sister, Jacobi, and I went scouting for the rental of chairs, tables, and dishes. As for the food, my sister's Québécois friends, Jacobi, Coco, Marc, and a few others, planned to take care of it. My sister had ordered chicken from a small Portuguese restaurant at the corner of Rachel and Clarke Streets, delicious charcoal-grilled chicken and other dishes from a caterer. This time, I did not bake my son's wedding cake myself. I was too tired, and the preparations were far from finished. So, we ordered the cake from a Portuguese bakery located at the corner of Duluth and Colonial Streets. Jacobi was in charge of decorating the two outdoor terraces.

So there was a lot to do, but in the end, everything was well organized.

In the meantime, my lawyer informed me that I had to appear in court regarding Jacques's case with the Société de l'assurance automobile du Québec. An agent from the Société would present the entire file before a judge on Friday, June 12, 1998, at 10 a.m., the day before my son's wedding. I had no choice; I promised my lawyer that I would be present in court.

Here is what I wrote in my journal on June 8.

June 8, 1998 Journal

Today, Monday, 5 days before Max's wedding, we have a lot to do. I haven't written for a week. I had no time. Yesterday, I helped my sister Irène with the big cleaning at her house. We are still tired, and we have 5 very busy days ahead of us. It is 6 o'clock in the morning, and my days start very early.

June 12, 1998 Journal

It is 10 o'clock in the morning, and I am at the courthouse. I am appearing in court regarding the divorce and other matters.

I am waiting! I think it is going to take a long time because the lawyer just told me that my case had been transferred to room 211.

My son is getting married tomorrow, June 13. I am preoccupied with all this. I don't know what is going to happen before the judge, and what lies or truths I will discover. I must stay positive; otherwise, I will break down.

I pray to God that everything goes well. I am still waiting. I trust, but at the same time, I feel a bit of fear. I came alone because all my loved ones were busy.

Part Four

The Wedding and the Trial

It rained throughout the entire wedding day. Jacobi had not at all imagined it would rain so much. Around 1 p.m., my loved ones bought plastic rolls to serve as a roof over the terrace. In the meantime, I went to Max's house to get dressed; it was I who had to drive Yole to the Anglican church, which was located on Sherbrooke Street West.

There were two priests, one Anglican and another Catholic. The wedding was celebrated in two languages, English and French. It was truly beautiful to see. What struck me the most was that at the very moment Yole entered the church, accompanied by her father, an intense expression radiated from my son's face his whole being was illuminated. Max was tapping his right foot, a gesture he makes when he is delighted. He had his warm, affectionate smile. Deep in my heart, I thought: *"I am so happy for him; he is happy and he loves this woman."*

That expression on his face was extremely important to me. I also felt good. I must mention that during the entire wedding, I did not have a single thought for Jacques. I was happy for my son.

Natasha had not come to the church because, at the same time, she was participating in a competition. Both events had been scheduled for the same day. As for me, I couldn't be in two places at once either.

For the competition in which Natasha was taking part, I had helped her a lot. She was supposed to come to the reception set for 6 p.m. at my sister's house. The church was packed with people, from both Max's side and Yole's.

The witnesses were a childhood friend of Max and a friend of Yole. Elle-Camay carried the rings. And the bridesmaids were Yole's two sisters and a cousin of Max. Members of our family from New York had come for the wedding.

At the end of the ceremony, the rain lessened in strength. When we arrived at Irène's, it was drizzling, and a few minutes later, everything became calm. The reception went well. I asked for a moment of silence in memory of Viviane, because I knew that in spirit she was among us. She was a woman full of humor who made us laugh so much, whether the circumstances were happy or sad. The newlyweds left at midnight, and the other guests continued the evening until 2 a.m. Young and old alike had a great time. My sister, Jacobi, and I went to bed at 5:30 in the morning. There was still a lot of food and drink left, which we shared among those present. The next day, people who had not been able to come the day before showed up. We received visitors all day Sunday. After all that, a big cleaning had to be done. My sister and I were totally exhausted. Irène had taken two weeks of vacation for the wedding.

As for me, I had not had any time at all to think about my day of June 12 at the courthouse. When the day of the hearing arrived, my heart was pounding and my hands were cold. I was having difficulty breathing. Maître Cardinal came to see me. He touched me on the left shoulder. He whispered to me, "Everything is going to be fine, don't worry." The SAAQ agent arrived shortly after.

In the meantime, I prayed fervently. My stress level was very high. At the same time, I was taking deep breaths.

The judge entered and sat down. My lawyer presented my case, and the judge asked us a few questions. Then he requested to hear the witness representing the SAAQ. When he began listing the compensations that the SAAQ had paid to Jacques, I felt as if I were in another world. From time to time, the judge would repeat this question to me: "Madam, are you okay?

Totally confused, I answered "yes" timidly, the sounds barely leaving my mouth. Jacques had received in all more than 100 thousand dollars in compensation and continued to collect an indemnity every 15 days. After hearing the testimony of the SAAQ agent, the judge ruled that the gentleman had to pay alimony of 100 dollars each month to the lady and half of the compensation money. The judge had asked about Jacques, and the lawyer informed him that the gentleman had gone to live in Haiti, taking all the money with him.

When we left the courtroom, my lawyer came up to me and whispered, "You had quite a shock, didn't you? Me too, I took one as well." He had not known that Jacques had pocketed so much money. But during a brief investigation, he had learned that my husband had tried to obtain a pension from the SAAQ. Personally, I told him, I did not want any pension; Jacques could very well keep all the money; I no longer wanted to have anything to do with the whole matter. Noticing that I was shivering, Maître Cardinal offered to drive me home. I declined the invitation, assuring him that everything would be fine. He accompanied me outside and waited until I got on the bus because that day, I had not taken my car. I had pain in my head and in my heart. A strong feeling of anguish gripped me. On the bus, I closed my eyes. I cried in silence. I was suffering inside. I repeated this prayer softly in my heart: "Jesus, Jesus, Jesus, come help me. Tomorrow is my son's wedding. Make it so that when I arrive at my sister's, I no longer feel sorrow. Help me, Jesus."

At my lawyer's suggestion, I had called my sister to give her an overview of how things had unfolded. Maître Cardinal wanted me to inform one of my loved ones that I was on my way. Just a few minutes after my arrival at my sister's, he phoned.

To check that I had arrived safely. He advised me to take good care of myself. My sister had prepared a verbena tea for me. I spoke to her briefly about what had happened in court, while making it clear that she should remain completely silent with my children, and especially with my son, whose wedding was imminent. In short, that is how I learned of this bad news on the very eve of my son's wedding, when I had absolutely no means to buy a gift for him and his wife.

In retrospect, I realized that every time the family experienced an important event, Jacques would distance himself. It had always been this way. Afterwards, he would use this excuse: "I know that your sister is always there to help you financially." If my sister helped us, it was because she did not want to see us suffer. I will never thank her enough for all she did for me and my children, unlike Jacques. After Max's wedding, I stayed for two weeks at my sister's.

Back to my journal.
June 21, 1998

It is 4:30 p.m., and I am staring at a blank page without knowing what to write about my son's wedding, my daughter's competition, and my appearance in court. There are so many things to say that I don't know where to begin. Everything rushes through my mind every day. I am currently at my sister's, sitting on the garden terrace. Since my son's wedding, I decided to spend a few days at her place to give Max and his wife the chance to be alone and have a proper honeymoon. I am staying with her temporarily because I have to move. I am eager because I want to get back to my own affairs.

Today is Father's Day. Natasha organized a dinner at a restaurant for Patrick. This morning, Patrick told me that he knew I was both a mother and a father. It was funny, and we laughed about it.

Chapter 6

Rue Saint-André in Plateau-Mont-Royal.

Part One

Moving to Rue Saint-André

I took possession of the apartment on the first of July. My sister and I went there to do some cleaning while waiting for me to move in, since I had not yet recovered all my furniture. The apartment was located five minutes from Irène's place. For me, that was convenient; I would feel less alone.

Back to my diary
July 4, 1998

It is noon. I am waiting for my sister Irène, with whom I will go run errands. I have been feeling a bit sad for two days. I don't know why. I have been having many nightmares.

My apartment is a 2½. It is not very big, but it is very clean. It is located on the ground floor. The laundry room is upstairs. It faces the street. My sister is helping me put everything in order. I am still sleeping at her place while waiting for the delivery of my bed and the few pieces of furniture I own, scheduled for Sunday.

Max landed a very good contract at Bombardier to design airplane interiors. I am happy for him.

As for me, I am more or less out of work. Let's just say that because of my accident, I can no longer work as before. I am waiting to be fully settled before looking again. I receive compensation from the CSST, but it is not enough to cover my needs.

I no longer think I will have a man in my life. I would be very demanding on this point, especially after all the bad experiences I have been through. These days, I think a lot about everything happening in the family because of Jacques. My children had an argument with my sister Irène because of him. They are so sensitive when it comes to me.

Max did not accept this. But I feel guilty, and I regret it. But Jacques is truly responsible. I will never forgive him for everything he did to us while he lived with us. He did everything he could to make us unhappy, to cause us pain. He was constantly plotting bad deeds. He claimed he did not feel responsible. As soon as he was no longer with us, he worked and put his affairs in order. To me, I was the person he most enjoyed making suffer.

Sometimes I had just finished cleaning, and he would manage to drop trash anywhere in the house. And he grumbled that it was up to me to clean up the dirt.

One day, Max confided this to me: "Mom, since I was little, I hear my father humiliate you by telling you to pick up all the things he left lying around and that it was your job. Mammy, if you knew how much that bothers me inside. Sometimes I want to hit him, but I don't, to protect you."

Tomorrow, July 5, is my daughter's birthday. I will not have any money to give her a gift. It's regrettable. With my apartment to pay for, and the phone and electricity, I no longer have money for food. That's why I need to find a small job. My sister helps me a little with food.

Back to the moving process

In the end, Max found friends to help with the move. It was July 6. The furniture company delivered the bed on July 7. I was able to sleep in my apartment and had a good night. I was delighted. The next morning, our friend Dédé came to paint the apartment. We had breakfast together. It was my first meal in the house.

After settling into my place, I became more stable. My daughter sometimes invited me to go to the beach with her and her family in Oka. Those little outings changed my mind. At times, bad memories resurfaced. Since I was living alone, I suffered. From time to time, I felt that I was not cut out to be alone in an apartment. I felt extremely vulnerable. The next moment, I judged that I had to hold on. At least I have a roof over my head. Stability became imperative for me. I lacked money, but I did not want to ask my sister or my children for any. I made them believe that everything was fine morally and financially.

The day after my son's wedding, I began to feel ill. I didn't mention it to my family so as not to worry them. I felt a pain on my left side, to the point that sometimes I wanted to open myself up to find what was causing the pain. Also, I still had headaches. In short, I was not well. Since my family doctor was on vacation, I called A Vietnamese doctor I used to consult when I lived on Boyer Street. Her clinic was located on Christophe Colomb Street near Beaubien Street.

After examining me, she sent me to have an electrocardiogram the same day at Jean-Talon Hospital. The next day, which was a Friday, her secretary called me to inform me that the doctor would like to see me the following Monday. I spoke vaguely about it to my sister. On Sunday morning, my sister suggested we go out for a walk. She then mentioned that I did not look well. She insisted on knowing what was wrong. I described my symptoms. They had not gone away. She decided to take me to the emergency room at Notre-Dame Hospital. I remembered that Vivanne had died in that hospital, and I feared they might decide to keep me there.

As soon as I arrived, I was examined by a doctor and received a serum injection while being given two aspirin tablets. After several tests, the results revealed that I was suffering from several health problems. Blood circulation was not functioning well; I had contracted an infection; my kidneys were slowing down. I was overwhelmed with extreme fatigue and fairly depressed. My stomach was not functioning normally, nor were my intestines. In short, my health was clearly failing. The solution: hospitalization. The next day, I was placed in a private room on the third floor, number 3014.

My sister had indeed done well to take me to the hospital, as I was beginning to lose touch with reality. I was going through extremely painful moments. I remember that at the end of July, I spent one night in unbearable pain. I thought I was losing my mind, I was suffering so much. I was really in bad shape.

I spent 18 days in the hospital. I slept a lot. When I returned home, I felt exhausted and fragile. Irène constantly took care of me. My sister Claire came back from Haiti with her husband and her grandson Samy for a one-month stay. During my convalescence, I did not write. I let my mind rest. During the stay of the visitors from Haiti, I made an effort to show them many neighborhoods in the city. I also agreed to accompany them to New York by bus. Irène could not have done it because of her work.

In New York, my brother-in-law Goslin, who is diabetic, suffered from excessive heat, to the point that his blood pressure and sugar levels dropped sharply. He became very weak. For the return to Montreal, we had to travel by car. One of my brothers who lived in New York drove us back in his magnificent, air-conditioned, brand-new Cadillac. My sister and her family were delighted with their stay in Montreal. After their departure for Haiti, I felt totally exhausted and drained of all energy.

11:30 p.m. I'll stop for tonight. I feel tired.
Good night.

December 28, 2006

Part Two

Jacques' surprise return to Montreal

At the beginning of September, precisely on September 5, 1998, I called Jacques' cousin. To my great surprise, it was he who answered. Without uttering a word, I immediately hung up. I did not expect to hear his voice, since he was supposed to be in Haiti. From this incident I concluded that he was acting hypocritically and that I had to remain on my guard.

I informed my children that Jacques had returned from Haiti. They urged me to exercise extreme caution, especially since I was still clearly vulnerable. I promised them I would make a real effort to be vigilant, while at the same time trying to ease their concern. Around September 11, Jacques called me to ask about my health. He told me that he had learned I was sick. We talked about everything and nothing. He offered to meet me. I flatly refused. I wanted to know how he had gotten my phone number. He admitted that he had gotten it from his cousin. Finally, he threw out this almost peremptory statement:
"Next time, I hope you'll accept a meeting because I have something to discuss with you about debts and the house." I replied, "We'll see."

He got into the habit of calling me every evening. When I saw his number on the caller ID, I didn't answer. But one evening, by mistake, I picked up the phone; he quickly told me that he had left several messages and that I hadn't called him back. I admitted that I should have, but that I had been very busy. He then suggested a meeting on September 12, 1998, stressing that it was very important.

The meeting was set for 3:00 p.m. at the McDonald's restaurant on Lajeunesse Street, near Henri-Bourassa.

The passage recounting this meeting appears in my journal. Here it is.

September 12, 1998   Journal

Report

I met Jacques at the Macdonald's restaurant on Lajeunesse Street at 3:00 p.m. I arrived 30 minutes early.

I was indecisive. I didn't know whether to stay or flee; I was torn by fear. As the minutes passed, my anxiety grew. The weather was nice that evening. I felt hot and cold at the same time. I stayed seated in my car parked in the lot, scanning every vehicle that arrived. I could feel my heart pounding. "I hope he didn't make me come all the way here for nothing," I thought. The next minute, I thought, "Enice, if he doesn't come, it's proof that it's better this way." At that moment, he appeared.

We shook hands and entered the restaurant. I was very nervous. I didn't know what to say; I didn't want him to notice my nervousness. In fact, he was nervous too, but he tried to hide it.

Here is how he started the conversation: "If I made you come here, it's to tell you that you already told me in January 1997 that you no longer loved me." Indeed, in June 1997, he had invited me to a restaurant. He had said that if I didn't love him, I needed to tell him directly. I had then decided: "It's true, Jacques,

"I no longer love you."

If he brings up this story today, it's for revenge; he thinks he can impress me with this argument from 1997. Back then, he never stopped hurting us. I decided that we would consider the whole matter from the beginning in order to get to the heart of the problem.

At first, we spoke calmly, and when the conversation began to get stormy, we agreed to return to one of the cars. There, things escalated again. Suddenly, I lunged at him, punching him and tearing his shirt. I kept telling him that I had wanted to hit him for a long time for everything he had done to me and the children. I couldn't stop. That said, I felt a sense of relief. He wanted to tell me what he had done over the past six months. I shouted at him that I hadn't come for that. When he began talking to me about the money he had received, I objected that the money had nothing to do with my real demands: "What I want is for you to leave me alone," and I stormed out of his car. Back in my vehicle, I stayed still for nearly 20 minutes. I was completely drained, yet I still felt a sense of calm.

When Jacques realized I was still there, he came over to ask if I was okay. I responded affirmatively. I left the place 10 minutes later. I realized he still wanted to get to me. His stubbornness reinforced my mistrust: "Enice, be careful. He's playing his game well."

Back at my home, I felt good. I was relieved of a heavy burden. He called to see if I was doing well. "Yes," I confirmed. He wanted to arrange another meeting, but I refused him.

In the meantime, I continued to function normally. I told the children that I had met Jacques. Their reaction was measured: "Mammy, you know what you have to do." Jacques began calling me frequently. Sometimes, I would accompany him to a restaurant. He claimed he had changed. He tried to make me feel guilty about the marriage and the money he had refused to give me. He justified himself by claiming that he had felt rejected when I had abruptly left the apartment in Montréal-Nord without warning. Furthermore, he said I had threatened to repay my sister with the money he would give me. Since he had abandoned a definitive plan of action, he preferred to flee Montréal and go to Haiti to find peace.

I let him speak, but I was highly skeptical. I actually had a little idea in the back of my mind. I decided to play along, remembering that nothing comes for free. Natatsha still warned me: "Mammy, you know my father, he's clever; you have to be careful, you've already suffered too much." Once again, I tried to reassure her and calm her worries.

On my birthday, October 1, 1998, a gesture he had never made before, he gave me a $100 gift check. I thanked him, but I still remained very cautious toward him.

Day by day, he showed me kindness. I still hadn't mentioned a word to my sister. I was waiting to see how things would unfold. I hadn't made love with him yet. I continued to observe him, but he realized that I was held back by fear. He had started coming to see me at home. But one evening, while we were talking about this and that, he eventually seduced me. Immediately afterward, I didn't feel happy. We discussed it and then cried together. He swore to me that he loved me and that he couldn't live without me. He claimed that the children didn't love him. "It's not that they don't love you," I objected. "It's that they saw me suffer too much. I am their mother; it hurts them to see that I am still unhappy because of you."

Present Moment

Friday, December 29, 2006

I know I have to continue the story of my experiences, but these days, it is quite difficult and painful for me. This part of my life that I am about to tell you already causes me suffering even before I begin to write it.

I don't know if I will be able to finish it. The truth is, I feel guilty and ashamed of myself. And above all, I am afraid of the judgment of others.

Reading what I had previously written in my journal made my heart ache. I don't understand how I let myself be taken in by him again and how I accepted doing things that did not at all resemble who I am. I called my daughter to explain all this to her. I cried all my tears, so ashamed of myself, so hurt. She reassured me, advising me not to give up, to continue my story for me, for her, for Max, and my grandchildren.

I continue my story

Jacques insisted that I stop the divorce proceedings and go live in Haiti with him. At first, I strongly resisted. I didn't fully trust him. I told him that I needed time to think. Here is the decision I recorded in my journal on October 5, 1998.

October 5, 1998

This morning, I prayed to God and asked Him to guide me in my actions, in everything I would do during the day. Especially regarding the decision about the divorce, and also my apartment. I wanted to know what to say to the lawyer and to the apartment owner if I were to leave.

I had the idea to contact Revenue Québec. An agent explained to me how to proceed to stop the separation. Since I had also called my lawyer, he returned my call. I already had the answer; I knew what to tell him. He asked me, "Are you sure you want to stop the separation proceedings?" I nodded. Everything had been going well for some time, and Jacques had changed a lot. Before hanging up, he reiterated his availability:

"Madame Toussaint, if you ever need me, I will be at your service. Good luck."

So it was done. I decided not to divorce or separate anymore. I would stay with Jacques for better or worse.

I called the lady in charge of the apartment; she agreed to rent it to someone else. I felt relieved. From now on, I had to carefully consider the future. And for that, I needed to have a serious discussion with Jacques.

Part Three

Resuming Couple Life, October 1998

I suggested to Jacques that he come to meet me so that we could discuss very important matters. My sister and my children had not yet been informed of my plans. I was really crazy to make such decisions. Anyway, I no longer knew what to think.

Jacques came that very evening. He wanted an immediate answer from me. I promptly made this point clear: "We need to have an honest discussion. You need to tell me why you want me to resume our life together. And above all, why you insist that I accompany you to Haiti." I also asked him if he was still seeing that woman from Toronto. He answered all my questions without hesitation. Regarding the divorce, he swore that he loved me and could not live with another woman but me. Concerning Haiti, he had a small business he wanted to manage with me, which would make us very happy. He had rented a house in Les Cayes, where he had installed all my furniture. As for the woman in Toronto, he no longer saw her. It was definitely over! He continued: "You can trust me; I am sincere."

I avoided committing too much: "Regarding Haiti, I am still thinking about it." Then I told him that I had already stopped the divorce. He thanked me. "Why are you thanking me?" I asked. He ignored the question. I brought up the financial matter. "Don't worry," he assured me, "the money is there. Together we will do good business in Haiti, if you agree to go with me." I revealed that I had personally devised a business plan for Haiti some time ago. Natatsha had initially had the idea. I then described my coffee business project to him, acknowledging that for the moment, I lacked some additional information and the necessary funds. He thought the idea was excellent. By the end of the meeting, he was hopeful that I would agree to accompany him to Haiti.

Days passed. He brought me suitcases and travel bags, in case I was finally ready. His calls became almost incessant. Meanwhile, I was secretly preparing another project. If I went there, it would only be for writing the first volume of my book, and for that purpose alone.

I invited Max and Natatsha to a restaurant to confide my intentions to them. Their reaction seemed very measured: "Mammy, if you feel this will be good for you, do it, but don't do it for him; think of yourself." Natatsha added: "Right now, you are very vulnerable. I hope he won't take advantage to try to seduce you. It's up to you to decide. I am against it. You must see for yourself. If you find it isn't right there, come back as soon as possible; we will be there for you." Max added: "I agree with Natatsha, but I am still worried for you, Mammy; we love you very much." All of this, with extreme gentleness.

I felt sorrow, though I didn't know why. I was still driven by this impulse to flee. It was stronger than me. At the same time, an inner voice ordered me: "Don't go, there is danger." I now know that I refused to listen.

Shortly after, Jacques returned to see me. We made love. He wanted to stay the whole night; I refused. Afterwards, I realized that I was not ready to forgive him. He was clearly trying to win me back. Instead of feeling proud, I felt sadness and anxiety. I thought about my children, my grandchildren, my sister, and my brother. But at the same time, I realized that they were now grown adults, and the little ones were well-raised by their parents. My sister and brother did not need me at all. Everyone was attending to their own matters, and I felt completely alone. I had to think of myself first. I resolved to do everything humanly possible to live in peace with Jacques, taking into account that time passes so quickly. Above all, I intended to live for myself and enjoy life. Moreover, I deemed it necessary to write my memoirs as soon as circumstances allowed.

It was the first time, I could hardly explain it that I reflected so deeply and seriously before making a decision. Fearing above all that I would eventually refuse, I asked him to give me space to continue my reflection.

One Sunday, he came to pick me up to take me to a flea market located between Saint-Léonard and Crémazie streets. After bringing me to the jewelry section, he bought a wedding ring for himself and one for me. He then whispered, "Here is my proof of love." At the time, I did not take it seriously. I had lost such precious possessions that this gesture left me absolutely indifferent. Regarding this, here is a passage from my journal.

October 15, 1997

Today, I stayed home to take stock. Upon waking, I felt a little lost, as if I had a memory lapse. I started to regain my senses around 11:30. Too many thoughts were crowding my mind, especially regarding the trip to Haiti.

I spent the day thinking about my project. I reflected on the good and bad aspects of the venture. After careful consideration, my decision is made. I will go to Haiti another time. I will return after winter. I know that God will guide me, because I will engage in many projects there.

Two weeks ago, I went back to the pawnshop to see if my jewelry was still there. They had sold everything. Back home, I thought about the sadness of the situation, then I decided to erase the memory of it. And I turned the page.

I no longer understand Jacques; he has said things whose meaning escapes me. He hides everything from me; I can feel it. He is afraid to tell me about his affairs. So I let him be. I don't think about it anymore; he knows what he wants. In any case, I have already made my decision.

I continue the story

I did my best to find another tenant for my apartment. I had already made a payment on my plane ticket. It was scheduled for December 2, 1998. Jacques would leave two weeks before me to be able to clear the container that would already have arrived there. He would come to pick me up at the airport.

I spent two weeks preparing my personal belongings that I planned to ship by container. Even at this stage of my project, I was still hesitant. I was not certain I had made the right decision. In the end, I paid for my plane ticket in full, concluding that I was taking this step for better or worse. Jacques, it is true, helped me with the payment for the ticket. Meanwhile, I wrote a letter to my sister and brother in which I informed them that I was going to Haiti to accompany Jacques and, above all, to write my book there. On the morning of October 2, I personally delivered the letter to them and explained in person the reasons for my trip. My sister remained silent. My brother wished me good luck.

I felt a sharp sorrow, knowing how much my decision grieved them. I felt deeply guilty, but the urgency to leave had become imperative. There was nothing I could do about it.

While waiting for my departure scheduled for December 2, I stayed at my daughter Natatsha's place. Jacques, meanwhile, had already left on November 4. During the month I spent at Natatsha's, I visited my sister several times. The atmosphere remained cold, but I understood her attitude. I still hadn't mentioned the subject of the disagreement. On the other hand,

I was able to enjoy the affection of my children and grandchildren. But I still didn't feel very stable. My feeling of desolation persisted. But I didn't want the children to notice. Finally, the big day arrived. I had no idea what awaited me there. In any case, I was no longer able to turn back. I had to stay positive and hope that everything would go well. A feeling of trust was essential.

Patrick drove me to Mirabel Airport. After passing through customs, I had breakfast. I was very pensive. I worried about my loss of energy. I boarded the plane, leaving Montreal and everyone I still loved behind for an adventure whose outcome I had no idea about. But I left everything in God's hands. Here is what I wrote about it in my journal.

December 2, 1998

I haven't written for quite some time. I've had a busy week. I worked a lot to prepare my luggage. I am on the plane. We left at 9:30, and it is now 11:55. I didn't have time to write earlier; I was too tired and slept a little during the trip. We've just been told that we are arriving at our destination. So, I will continue writing in Haiti. I leave everything in Jesus' hands.

Chapter 7

Third Return to Haiti

Part One

A Disastrous Arrival at Jacques' Sister's

December 2, 1998

At the airport, it was Jacques who came to pick me up, accompanied by my niece Yolaine's young boy, as she could not leave work. The airport was crowded with people. I felt dizzy and exhausted; the trip had drained me. It was extremely hot. Jacques claimed that the young boy was his little servant. I found him cold and distant. He didn't speak much. I asked if he planned to take me to my niece's place in the plain, as usual.

"No," he grumbled, "I'm taking you to my sister Raymonde's in Delmas."

This was not at all our plan, but he would hear nothing of it. He also told me that the next day he would leave for Les Cayes, but I would not go with him. He would drop me off with my belongings at his sister's in Miragoâne and would only come for me when he was ready but not before, because he had important matters to settle first.

His sister welcomed me warmly, but I did not feel at all comfortable. I felt out of place, exhausted, and almost destroyed. She offered me something to drink, but I declined since I had brought my own water. She invited me to eat. I thanked her, pretending I was not hungry. I felt like a stranger among these people. She lived on the lower floor of a house with a parking area. The apartment included a bathroom, a living room, a dining room, a kitchen, and three bedrooms. Everything was clean and simple.

Jacques noticed my distress: "Let's take a walk," he suggested.

He took me to a restaurant on Delmas Street. He told me I needed to eat, or I would get sick and even weaker. But I was still waiting for a proper explanation, which never came. He kept urging me not to worry and assured me he would come back to get me in Miragoâne, specifying that my stay there would only last a few days. But each time, the conversation shifted to a new version of events.

At the height of my impatience, I demanded that he take me immediately to my niece's place to sleep and come for me the next day. He claimed he had to be at customs at five in the morning for clearance operations.

Resigned, I agreed to return to his sister's since I had no other choice. I confided to her and her husband the full extent of my distress regarding the thorny issue of Les Cayes. They appeared very surprised. I must note that since my arrival in Haiti, Jacques was no longer the affectionate and considerate man I had hoped to find. He had returned to the man he truly was before and even worse.

While raising his voice, he also addressed the matter bluntly: "There's a young girl living with me." At that moment, I was speechless. Within seconds, I imagined myself back in Montreal, overwhelmed with shame in front of my children, my sister, my brother, all my family, and my friends. I immediately went into the room that Jacques' sister had made available to us. I opened my bag and took out a box of antidepressants. I swallowed all 30 pills at once. Jacques could only witness the scene. He then put his fingers in my mouth trying to remove the pills. I bit him while shouting at him to leave me alone.

I only remember that the three of them were staring at me, calling out loudly. I asked them to let me rest. I was still fully dressed. I don't know who managed to undress me. It seems that the next morning, Jacques tried unsuccessfully to wake me. The three of them also tried to get me out of bed, but I kept falling back. Jacques finally left, leaving me in the care of our hosts, citing customs procedures and an imminent business trip to Les Cayes. I slept through the entire day. The couple did not deem it necessary to notify my children in Montreal or my family members living in Port-au-Prince. I should note here that I had promised my children I would call them either the evening or the morning after my arrival in Haiti.

Since Natatsha had not heard from me, she called my niece Yolaine, who herself did not know what had happened to me. Panic gripped the family. Natatsha phoned Jacques' sister in Port-au-Prince to check if she had news of me. She informed her that I was at her place, sleeping. Natatsha asked to speak to her father, but she said he had left for Les Cayes. She was very upset: "What do you mean, Mother is at your place?" This led to the following exchange: "Your mother isn't well. What do you mean? I want to speak to her." Jacques' sister, Raymonde, then woke me up. Later, my daughter told me that at that time, I could barely speak; I was murmuring words she couldn't understand.

Raymonde took the phone again, and Natatsha urged her to take me to the hospital as quickly as possible. I only learned about all these events the following day. It was very late when we returned from the hospital.

Jacques' sister told me that I had taken a box of pills. I went to check the contents of the box: it was empty. She strongly advised me to resist sleep, even though I felt an overwhelming urge to do so. She came to lie beside me to keep me awake. She talked a lot, while my mind My mind remained confused. She would call my name from time to time. Her husband tried to reach Jacques, but in vain. The next day, my brother came to get me at the request of my sister Irène and my daughter. As soon as I arrived at his place, I called Natatsha. I made her believe that I had a drop in blood pressure and that I was feeling better.

I had never admitted to anyone that I had attempted suicide. I was too ashamed. Raymond and her husband were too afraid to talk about it, as was Jacques. I only confessed it to my daughter a year later. She was speechless. She shouted at me: "You actually went that far, oh! Mammy, you really suffered." To which I replied, "I don't want to talk about it anymore; we should just forget this story."

I spent two days at my brother's place in Delmas 31 and was able to recover a little. Jacques had called his sister, Raymonde, to inform her that he would come to pick me up. The day before his return, my brother Alain brought me back to Raymond. The next morning, Jacques took me to my sister's in Miragoâne.

If I attempted suicide (it's a strong word), it was not truly for Jacques far from it. It was because I had abandoned everyone I loved to follow him. I was so ashamed of myself. I had nothing left. I had reached rock bottom. I refused to turn back, even though the children urged me to return to Canada. I pretended to them that, since my plane ticket was valid for two months, I would take the opportunity to rest at my sister's in Miragoâne. My return date was, in reality, uncertain. To be honest, I was in complete despair. I had no one to confide in. I couldn't even cry anymore. My situation was heartbreaking.

Jacques took me to Miragoâne. During the two-hour-and-thirty-minute journey, we barely spoke. After all, what was there to say? When we arrived at our destination, he gave me some money for my living expenses. Then he almost immediately set off again toward Les Cayes, vaguely promising that he would return soon to bring me some food supplies. I found myself alone in a city I no longer recognized, so changed. But I realized that I had no choice but to adapt to this environment.

Part Two

Life in Miragoâne

December 1998

I arrived in Miragoâne on October 10. I was staying with my sister Claire and her husband Goslin, who had two young domestic helpers in their service. The house had two floors. At the front of the first floor, there was a small shop. A second room served as a storage area for goods and led to a staircase that went up to the second floor. In this same room, every Wednesday, Claire organized a prayer meeting with her Protestant sisters. I myself participated several times.

Another room served as a small indoor kitchen, while outside there was a traditional-style kitchen, a space for washing, and latrines.

On the second floor, there was a living room with a balcony in the front, overlooking the street. From this balcony, one could watch the passersby and the small merchants quarreling over trivial matters. The street was bustling with activity, and in the heart of the city, businesses were very prosperous. The second floor also included two bedrooms, a dining room, and a bathroom. My sister had arranged a garden on the roof of the outdoor kitchen. She had also installed a water cistern on the roof of the house.

The house was located on Bord-de-Mer Street. My cousin Fabienne, Vivianne's sister, had lived just across the street a year earlier. I often went to talk to her to pass the time. Now that she had passed away, I had no one to communicate with. I still had my friend Nélia, who lived on Bel-Air Street, at the top of the town, about a 20-minute walk from Claire's house. She was a long-time friend. She lived in a large house with her husband Stone. Their home was pleasant, perched on the hill. I also spoke quite often with my brother-in-law Goslin and my sister Claire.

My sister and her husband welcomed me warmly into their home. I felt comfortable, and they made every effort to facilitate my stay. Here is an excerpt from my journal on the subject.

Saturday, December 12, 1998

The day of my arrival, December 10 at 3 p.m., I went to visit my good friend Nelia that same evening on Bel-Air Street. Then I returned to Claire's. Since Thursday evening, there had been no electricity in Miragoâne. It was dark, and there were many mosquitoes. Fortunately, Mirtha, Claire's daughter, had brought me a mosquito net, at least so that those little creatures would leave me in peace.

The next evening, the electricity was back, but there was no fan and no television. I was living in primitive conditions. We were exposed to heavy infestations and foul odors in Miragoâne. The sewers polluted the air. I feared catching a disease. I hardly slept that night; I kept thinking about my life and how Jacques was treating me. I didn't understand anything anymore; I vaguely sensed that I was once again caught in one of his traps. I asked Jesus why, since I was an entirely innocent woman.

He made me leave Canada to accompany him to Haiti, to show me his love, and now he is indifferent and contemptuous toward me. I will not let myself be crushed. I have to do what I came here to do, and after that, we will see.

Tonight, I am going to my friend Nelia's to tell her a bit about my problems; otherwise, I will suffocate, for I have too many things on my mind. She will help me find a solution. I do not think I can stay in Miragoâne for very long; in any case, the future will tell the rest.

I continue my story

Since I have been in Miragoâne, I have had no news from Jacques. Yet he knows that my situation is difficult: no electricity, no water, and I had almost no money left. I do my best, however, to fill my days. My pastime is writing; I describe what I observe around me and my environment. In Montreal, I had bought notebooks and fountain pens for writing, and a book that explains how to write one's memoirs. It is fascinating. I spend hours taking notes and making a plan for executing my writing project. To distract myself, I chat with my brother-in-law or watch the passersby. Sometimes, in the afternoons, I go visit my friend Nelia.

Ten days passed, and still no news from Jacques. I then tell my brother-in-law of my intention to go to Les Cayes to see what is happening there. He advises me not to do it, but to call Jacques to find out the reason for his silence.

The next day, December 19, I set out to call him very early on the telephone. After many difficulties, I finally reached him. The connection, very poor, was brief. He promised to come see me the following Sunday.

Back from the phone call, to clear my mind, I sit on the balcony at the back of the house, facing the upper part of the town. From there, I can see everything happening on Bel-Air Street; I can also enjoy a fresh breeze it is a healthier and calmer place. There, I no longer hear the street vendors shouting at each other. There, I can write, read, and say my prayers.

That day, here is what I recorded in my journal.

December 19, 1998 – Journal

I am sitting on the back balcony of my sister Claire's house. It is 10:45 a.m. The sky is blue with a few clouds. The weather is beautiful, and I can see Bel-Air Street. I look at the houses built one above the other on the hillside. It feels as if all these houses might tumble down toward the lower part of the town. What catches my eye the most is the house of the nuns across Bel-Air Street, where I used to go to school and lived as a boarder. It looks like an abandoned house. Yet it still functions. But it is no longer the Notre-Dame-de-Lourdes school. The nuns are no longer there; it has been transformed into a secondary school for young girls run by laypeople.

From the balcony, I could make out the windows of the bedrooms. For example, Sister Berthe's room, where I used to go very often. From the balcony of that room, I could overlook the northern side of the town (the lower fort area), the place where the soccer field used to be. I could see the room where I slept with two other girls. There were three of us per room. I could also make out the dormitory in the back, where we gathered after Sister Jean turned off the lights. We would meet there to talk, eat, and watch through the back window the boys who came to sing for us at the calvary (the side where a cross is perched) not far from the school.

This is a part of my life I will never forget. There was a whole group among my classmates, particularly Josie, who was my best friend. She passed away in 1995. Since that day, my life has changed. I will explain this part of my life on another occasion. At the present moment, I am not ready.

"If I have included these moments in my book, it is to show that despite my problems, I took the time to create little moments of happiness for myself so that I could continue living."

Let's continue my story.

Jacques was supposed to come see me on Sunday, December 20.

That day, I waited for him in vain. I tried everything not to appear angry. I didn't want those around me to notice my distress, but I also didn't want to continue suffering any longer. I made a conscious effort to focus on something else. That night, I had terrible nightmares. I tried to push them away to avoid feeling too much pain.

The next morning, I went to visit my good friend Nelia. I spent the day and the night at her place. Before going to bed, I took a long shower, because at her house there was light and running water. She had a generator. The breeze from a fan helped me sleep well, and the next day, I returned to my sister's house.

Part Three

My Joyful Christmas in the Countryside

Jacques arrived on the morning of December 23, 1998. He apologized for not coming on Sunday and for not being able to answer the phone to inform me. He offered to accompany me to Port-au-Prince, where we would spend the night before returning to Miragoâne on the eve of December 24.

After a moment of reflection, I accepted his proposal. In Port-au-Prince, I stayed at his sister's place. We barely had time to have lunch in a restaurant because he was in a hurry to go buy parts for his van. We were traveling in my car, which he had just cleared through customs, as his van was having mechanical problems. On December 24, around noon, we left Port-au-Prince to return to Miragoâne.

In the meantime, I had mentioned that I would be bored in Miragoâne at Christmas, since there was no electricity. I planned to go to my friend Nelia's house. He thought that was a good idea. Ultimately, when we arrived at the Carrefour des Ruisseaux, as it was getting late, Jacques told me that he would take me to Les Cayes with him instead of dropping me off at Nelia's. He would drop me off at his sister Renate's, who was arriving from Philadelphia to spend the holidays with her mother in Haiti. Upon our arrival in Les Cayes, he promised to communicate without fail with my sister Claire to ease her worries.

The trip did not go as planned. There were tire punctures. To get to Renate's mother's house, we had to take a bumpy, muddy road. The car got stuck. It was hell, completely dark, with no houses nearby. I feared the intrusion of thieves or malicious strangers. Fortunately, two men who were passing by came to help Jacques. In those circumstances, I could do nothing but wait. We also had to cross a river on foot and walk for 20 minutes in the dark. My God, it was painful! In the end, we arrived at our destination exhausted and dirty.

When we got to Renate's, we learned that she was absent. She had gone to town to attend Mass and was expected to return the next day. It was her mother who welcomed us. She obviously knew Jacques. She did not recognize me, as I had only met her once.

She was in a wheelchair. She was hosting a young woman with her 7-year-old child. She was very welcoming. For them, we were distinguished visitors. It was 10:30 PM, very late for people in the countryside. The lady's name was Louise. She asked Jacques if he would stay overnight. "No, not me," he replied, "but my wife will stay to meet Renate tomorrow." She immediately advised him to leave without delay, as the road was not at all safe at night. Then, speaking directly to me, she affirmed that I was in good hands at her home. She added, "You are at home here; my daughter's friends are my children too." Her words reassured me, and I felt at peace. I therefore confirmed to Jacques that it would be best for him to set off immediately. He kissed me on the forehead and left.

After his departure, I realized that I was in the outskirts of Les Cayes, among people I did not know, on the eve of Christmas, far from my children and my family. That is when I started to cry. My hosts did not understand why I was sobbing so much. They themselves thought they were the cause. I informed them that they had nothing to do with it, but without explaining further. At that moment, the lady told me, "When an adult cries, it is because there is something sad inside them and in their heart." Her remark comforted me, and I timidly smiled.

I discreetly observed their faces, the faces of simple people who lived in the countryside. There was joy in their eyes. Even though they lacked electricity and comforts, they were happy. It made me reflect.

I judged that if I had ended up in the countryside, in this peaceful place to spend Christmas, there was certainly a reason, with the good Lord always measuring His decisions. I felt better from then on and was no longer sad. The mistress of the house (everyone obeyed her orders) had the occupants of the neighboring dwelling summoned.

She told them that she had special visitors and that they should come celebrate. They came, full of cheer. We drank Haitian cola and ate biscuits. The moon was full, and the night was beautiful. I looked at the stars. I spoke about my children and grandchildren to my new friends. I showed them a photo of my little family. They were happy, and so was I.

At midnight, I went outside to observe the sky again. I prayed and wished my children, my sister, and my brother a Merry Christmas. I thanked God. I was not sad. When I returned, the mistress of the house told me that I would sleep in her daughter's room and invited me to behave as if I were at home. She let me know that she had put water in the room so that I could wash. I thanked her and retired, saying goodnight to everyone. One thing struck me upon my arrival: the absence of mosquitoes. I slept well, having suffered no bites from those little insects or their irritating buzzing in my ears. Moreover, it was not hot. In short, a very comfortable situation. I was eager for the next day to admire the outdoors, nature, and the surroundings.

The next morning, upon waking, I hurried outside. I looked at the plain covered with green grass, trees, and rice and banana plants. It was all so beautiful. The house was surrounded by gardens and vegetation of all kinds. There were other houses in this large yard. Nature was fresh and lovely. There was no risk of pollution. Further away, there was a large river and a clear stream where people came to fetch water.

The house itself, impressively clean, had two bedrooms, a living room that also served as a dining area. One room served as storage and another as a room for the housekeeper. The kitchen was at the back of the house along with the latrines. At the front of the house stretched a large terrace, and next to it, a large, deep basin sheltering giant trees. All of this gave a vision tinged with mysticism. Still in the yard, one could see a small house containing little cauldrons, small jugs, candles, etc. Apparently, it was the mystical dwelling of a former president of Haiti (Antoine Simon).

Such an attractive site should be a tourist spot, but it is quite far from the city. To reach it, one must leave their vehicle and continue the rest of the journey on foot for nearly 20 minutes. The occupants of the house served me coffee and bread. I, for my part, gave them money to buy food items to prepare a hot and appetizing meal for everyone. A few moments later, other warm neighbors came to greet me. I was torn between joy and sadness. I noticed gestures I had never seen elsewhere. I took pleasure in observing the comings and goings and the behaviors of all these people. I amused myself by following with my eyes the dogs running in the yard, the horses, the donkeys grazing, and so on. It was wonderful. I breathed in the fresh air.

It was noon, and Jacques had not yet returned. Internally, I was annoyed by his delay. But at the same time, I was happy to be far from the city's pollution. And I was in the company of sincere people.

Renate arrived before Jacques. Learning that he had left me with people I did not know, she had worried. Upon her arrival, she seemed surprised to see me in good spirits among all these people. "Who do you think you are?" her mother shouted. "I know how to receive guests! I am a great lady." She added, "This woman is a good person; she does not look down on others. I like her." Her daughter burst out laughing, and everyone else followed suit. Jacques finally arrived around 2:00 p.m. His two nephews, whom I was meeting for the first time, had arrived earlier. They told me many anecdotes about him. In this way, I learned everything I wanted to know about him.

I thus spent Christmas Eve and my day on December 25 among strangers. We talked at length. At the same time, I thought a lot about my children. It saddened me not to be able to speak with them. Yes, I felt comfortable with these people for the occasion, but they were not part of my family. Upon his arrival, I asked Jacques to take me to the telephone office so I could call my children and my sister. I also wished to return to Miragoâne on December 26 without delay. He immediately agreed. The presence of all these people seemed to embarrass him. His sister scolded him for having brought me there, far from everything. He did not react.

He took me to the telephone office, but I could not reach anyone as the phone system was defective. To make up for it, we went to a restaurant, after which he brought me back to his sister's country house. We had a heated discussion about the way he had treated me. He kept repeating that he loved me and asked me to wait until he managed to get rid of the girl he was seeing. I was supposed to understand that in Haiti, things do not work like in Montreal. People often try to get revenge by resorting to black magic. He told me that when he settled in the neighborhood, the young girl, who was in secondary school, lived with her mother and two other children in a house that had only one room. The family, extremely poor, lived without electricity.

My partner had a generator that supplied him with electricity day and night. His porch was illuminated by a fairly powerful electric bulb. The student and her classmates would come to study in the evening on the porch under the light of this bulb. This is a common practice in Haiti: young people whose parents do not have access to electricity go to study in parks or on neighbors' porches equipped with the precious current. This adolescent, who was younger than our daughter Natatsha, quickly learned that Jacques had arrived from Canada and that he was "a diasporan." She rushed to befriend my husband's nephews. She lamented that there was nothing to eat at her home and begged him to intervene on her behalf with Jacques. He agreed to feed her daily, so to speak. The same was then done for the whole family. She occasionally came to watch television. Gradually, at Jacques' instigation, she left school and moved in with him. He had promised to teach her many other things. Her mother quickly approved the new arrangement.

All these details, and many more, were provided to me by the girl's own sister. In Haiti, poverty and destitution force many people into all sorts of compromises. Jacques, for his part, never gives anything for free. He took advantage of the young girl's vulnerability to turn her into a sexual slave. He had transported all my furniture to Haiti. The adolescent, transformed into an adult woman, used it as if it belonged to her, especially since her lover had sworn to her that he was divorced and that he himself had purchased most of that furniture.

Returning to the evening of December 25, Renate and I spent the night in her room. We talked at great length. She told me everything my husband had already recounted to me, and even more. The next day, he came to pick me up to take me to the bus station. He paid extra so that I could sit in the front seat, next to the driver and two other passengers.

Leaving Les Cayes, I had told Jacques that I would go to Port-au-Prince toward the end of December to confirm my return ticket to Montreal; otherwise, I would lose it. Alternatively, I would call to confirm it in Montreal in January. "If ever you cannot communicate with them by "Call me on the phone; I will take you to Port-au-Prince," was his reply.

I left Les Cayes with a bit of regret, especially at leaving Mrs. Louise and her small family. I had given them some money as a gift, as well as to Jacques' nephews. I felt good with them; I loved that place. The air was fresh and pure. I slept peacefully. As I departed, I had the feeling that one day I would return there. It was simply a feeling, nothing more.

I allow myself the modest reflection that follows:

I had the feeling that I had gone there for a mission. For me and for them. Quiet people welcomed me into their home for a sad Christmas without gifts, without money, with just a little food to share. There was little hope for much. And I arrived destitute, with a sad heart ready to falter, without my children by my side, following the steps of a man who caused me pain.

I cried. They advised me with their gentleness and the joy in their eyes; their dedication brought happiness back into my heart. And I was able to share that happiness with them by transmitting the care and love owed to my children and grandchildren. I gave them money as a gift so they could eat and celebrate Christmas. I was delighted to see them happy. I was happy too. At midnight, when I went outside to pray, observing the stars, I felt the presence of my little family. I had said thank you to Jesus. These people had needed me, and I had needed them. Thank you, Jesus.

Part Four

My Return to Miragoâne After a Joyful Christmas

Upon my arrival in Miragoâne, my sister and her husband were waiting for me. I told them about my adventure, and they were left speechless listening to me speak. Since it was the holiday season, I gave my sister a hand in her business. I was mainly active on the lower floor of the shop with her. People came to buy, and I arranged them in a line because everyone wanted to buy and pay at the same time. Even her husband and a servant came to help us. Before December 31, 1998, she had sold a lot. She told me that it was I who had brought her this luck. I was delighted for her. I tried to call Port-au-Prince to confirm my plane ticket, but the communication to Port-au-Prince, as well as to Montreal, was not working. I was stressed and sad, stressed about the ticket and sad for my family, who had not heard from me for several days. I was able to reach Jacques in Les Cayes. He promised that he would come to pick me up to take me to Port-au-

Prince on the morning of December 28. In the end, he did not come. The deadline being December 29, I had evidently lost my return ticket. I was very angry. I resigned myself to staying in Miragoâne for a while. I did not yet know what I would do next.

My friend Nelia's children had come from Montreal to spend the holidays with her. She was very happy about it. Her daughter and her husband came to see me at my sister's. They found the city dirty and repulsive. That evening, the smell of the sewers was terribly strong. They asked me why I agreed to live in such an unhealthy place. If I did not leave, they predicted, I would certainly catch a disease. I told them that I had a plan. In January, I intended to put it into action. They did not stay long. Upon leaving, they advised me to take good care of myself. Their return date to Montreal was January 4. I went to see them. I gave them letters addressed to my children and my sister.

In the end, Jacques showed up on January 1. He claimed that his car had experienced problems, that the telephone system was defective, and that he had not been able to call me. Knowing well that he was giving excuses, I did not react. He planned to leave the following afternoon. I told him that, because of him, I had probably lost my ticket. I also asked him this question: "I would like to know what you want from me, why all these mysteries."

His response was immediate: "You say you want to be independent, you want to fly on your own, so why don't you ask your sister Claire for your share of the inheritance, the one your father left at his death?" I immediately replied: "No, I cannot do such a thing! That inheritance does not interest me. Besides, two years ago, I did not even know it existed!"

He retorted: "Well, you have a fortune and you prefer to live in misery out of simple respect for people. I do not understand it." He continued: "You are not going to steal; your share belongs to you, you just have to divide the land and give their shares to your brothers and sisters." He added, "There is only one person benefiting. Yet there is your mother's house on the main street and your father's house in Nouvelle Citée." I asked him how to go about the division. He replied: "If you want, I will lend you money to hire a notary and a surveyor. They will do everything for you." He repeated again: "Don't forget, you are within your rights."

"I will look into it," I said. "I will think about the matter, then I will speak to my brother-in-law, then to my sister to ask her for the papers of the lands and houses." The next day, before his departure, he left me money in case I decided to consult a notary and a surveyor and to obtain legal documents. He repeated that the telephone in Les Cayes had not been working since before Christmas. He would have to go to Port-au-Prince. He would come pick me up. Then he left. We had reached January 2, 1999.

As soon as he left, I went to join the family for the January 2 meal. Claire's children came with their children and spouses to spend New Year's Day and January 2 with their parents. The atmosphere was festive. We had fun. I had a good time. The next day, they returned to Port-au-Prince, and everything became as before. On New Year's Day, the city had been cleaned; it remained calm for two days. But, from January 3 onward, everything resumed as before.

My Journal

January 4, 1999

It is 3 o'clock in the morning; I cannot sleep. I decided to cross the living room to write so as not to disturb my loved ones.

I took a candle to light my way. I am alone; I make no noise. I hear only the ticking of the clock.

I have been here for a month waiting for Jacques. I do not know for how long, and for me, it is urgent because I have matters to settle here. After reviewing my affairs, I think there will be many changes here as well as in Canada. I have the impression that Jacques would like me to stay alone without family around me. Before, it was my sister Irène who was the thorn in his side. Now, it is my daughter Natatsha. Yet, these two never bothered us. They only wanted what was good for me, that's all.

One thing I know is that I regret coming to Haiti, thinking that Jacques was sincere. I was mistaken once again. If I had known that he was living with a young girl, I would not have come to Haiti. Now, I am here; I stay to settle my affairs, and I must write my book at all costs.

Part Five

My Steps for the Division of Land or Property

On the morning of January 5, 1999, I went to my friend Nelia's house to greet her children before their departure for Canada. Then I went to visit two former teachers, Mariette and Daniella. I shared a good time with them. Afterwards, I dyed my sister Claire's hair. I took the opportunity to talk to her about the division of the land and the documents. She was on the defensive. She believed that a family meeting was necessary. She thought that if I acted this way, it was certainly at someone's instigation. She advised me to be cautious. She emphasized that it was necessary to wait for the responses of all the other heirs.

I informed her that my decision was already made: all the heirs will be informed; I would write a letter to each of them. She said to me: "You've done your homework!" I acknowledged that I had already discussed it with a notary. She discussed it with her husband. Two days later, she gave me all the documents.

On January 6, 1999, Jacques came to pick me up to take me to Port-au-Prince. This time, I warned him that I would not go to his sister's house. We went to stay at my niece Yolaine's place. We spent two days there. I felt very comfortable. There was water and electricity. I took a shower every day, morning and evening, and I enjoyed it. My hosts had an artesian well in their yard. Upon our return to Miragoâne, we brought water for my sister. The water was good to drink, but one still had to be careful. As a precaution, I did not drink it.

Everything was going well with my sister and brother-in-law. I went to the Church of God every Sunday with her. Her Protestant sisters liked me. Every Wednesday, I attended their prayer meeting at her house. I also accompanied her to cooperative meetings where different topics were discussed: community services, consumer services, etc. The organization, which had over 480 members, seemed very efficient to me. There was no deficit in their accounts. I asked for the floor to congratulate them, particularly the president of the association.

In the meantime, I continued my steps for the division of the property. On Thursday, January 11, I applied for an identity card at the Tax Services; afterward, I went to Téléco to call Jacques. Communication was not possible. I wanted to keep him informed of the progress of the formalities.

The next day, I went to present the documents to the notary. He gave me a price and requested a deposit, as did the surveyor. I gave them the little I had left, hoping to reach Jacques as soon as possible.

During my stay in Miragoâne, to manage to sleep, I had to take Ativan. Since I could not reach Jacques, I took the bull by the horns and made an incredible move that even today, I still find almost unimaginable. You will discover what it was by reading my memoirs and my journal.

Chapter 8

My Incredible Saga with My Double

Part One

An "Untimely" Appearance in Les Cayes

Don't judge me, because even I don't understand it. In my view, it wasn't really me acting this way. It was very likely the other Enice secretly resurfacing. I was no longer myself. I could no longer contain it. The other one was taking over completely.

Living in Miragoâne was becoming increasingly difficult for me. No communication, no electricity, no water. I couldn't reach my children, and I had started to get sick because of the unsafe water. I suffered from itching all over my body. The town was excessively polluted and horribly dirty. I couldn't even wash my clothes. Yet, Jacques had everything at his disposal at Les Cayes.

My Journal

January 19, 1999

It is 6:30 p.m., I am in Les Cayes in Jacques' office I can call it our office.

I have been sitting with my planner open in front of a blank page for two hours. I can't find the words to describe how I managed to get here today. It's quite an event. I don't know how to explain it. I realized that it was easier to take action than to prescribe it.

Yes! I am with my husband, Jacques. I have taken my rightful place since January 14, 1999. I am going to recount what has happened over the last five days. It's sheer madness so far. I can't believe it!

Let us resume my story

It was Tuesday, January 10, 1999. I was in Miragoâne. I went to Téléco to call Jacques to inform him about the progress of the property division. But the telephone system was still down. I had not heard from him since January 1. Yet, I had a lot to tell him. I also needed him for the surveying of the family land.

I then thought that I should go directly to Les Cayes. I felt it was wise to share my intentions with my friend Nélia. When I arrived at her place, she was taking a nap. I told the servant not to wake her. I decided to stop by the neighbor, Anne, while waiting for her to wake up. Anne seemed delighted with my visit. As the conversation got going, I explained my situation. I told her that Jacques wanted me to stay in Miragoâne while he tried to get rid of a young woman who had settled in his house.

She immediately reacted: "My little girl, you are innocent. I'm going to tell you the story of a friend who lives in New York." She continued: "You know, her husband and she built a big house in Port-au-Prince. The husband returned to the country, claiming he was going to prepare the way. He took a young woman as his mistress, and now that my friend also wants to return, he tells her all kinds of threats to discourage her." Then she concluded: "It's a very good idea to spend the weekend in Les Cayes at a hotel. That way, the girl will feel the pressure. Even if he asked you to wait, go to Les Cayes anyway, but not to his house." I thanked her for the advice and returned to my friend Nélia, who gave me the same advice as her neighbor. Since it was getting late, I went back to my sister Claire's house. I immediately informed my brother-in-law, Goslin, that I was leaving for Les Cayes to meet Jacques. He approved my plan.

The next morning, Wednesday, January 11, I packed a small suitcase. I went to settle my affairs with the surveyor. Since my friend Nélia had come to see me, I told her about my departure for the next day,

Thursday, January 12. I informed my sister that I was leaving for Les Cayes the following day. That night, I hardly slept. I was eager for daylight.

Upon waking at 4:30 a.m., I said a long prayer. After having a hot coffee, I was ready to depart. Claire and Goslin thought it was too early. I told them it was better for me. I asked them to pray for me, then I got into the van heading to Ruisseaux. From there, I took another vehicle bound for Les Cayes.

While boarding the bus, I felt no fear. I felt strong. I asked Jesus to guide me so that I could make a good decision.

During the entire journey, I had the impression that I was no longer myself Even. A voice whispered to me: "You will not go to the hotel, you are going to Les Cayes to your home, to take your place and your belongings, it is your right." I tried to resist this voice. But a mysterious authority pushed me to obey it. It was stronger than me. I had become a completely different woman.

When I arrived at the bus station in Les Cayes, I asked the driver how to get to the second main street. He told me, "Madam, you just need to take a taxi," the taxi being a motorcycle. Since I only had a small suitcase, I indeed took a taxi that dropped me off in front of Jacques' house; it was 11:30 in the morning.

I found my husband in his store, standing and performing an electrical repair. The young girl was reading, seated at a desk. When Jacques saw me, he reacted like someone who had been expecting me. I greeted him. He calmly asked what was going on. He led me to the dining room. I replied that if I had decided to come, it was because I couldn't get through on the phone. He suggested waiting for two minutes. Then he extended this invitation: "I have to run an errand for Renate's mother; come with me." I pointed out that I had not come to Les Cayes to visit Renate's mother in the countryside. I added that if I agreed to accompany him, I would leave my suitcase in the house.

He went in to drop off the suitcase. He added, "I will be more at ease to talk to you on the way and at Louise's." Upon our arrival there, in the presence of Renate's mother, I told Jacques: "I have come to take my place. I will not go back to live in Miragoâne." He froze.

Renate's mother then intervened: "Jacques, your wife has come to stay in her home, this is her place, it is up to you to do things properly." He replied: "Madam, I am an adult, I am the one who must know what to do." We stayed there a few minutes, then we went to sit on the edge of the beach to continue our conversation.

We discussed the situation. He finally decided to act. I was calm, and it felt good to come to the seaside to breathe the fresh air. The sound of the waves and the silence of nature comforted me. I was ready for whatever was about to happen.

Around 5:30 p.m., we returned to Jacques' place. The young girl was upstairs with her sister at that time. Jacques had supper, but I didn't take anything, not even water. The young girl and her sister came down from the upper floor. They entered the shop and spoke very loudly, using vulgar language. Jacques went to join them; he put the sister out the door and went upstairs with the girl to talk to her about leaving the house. She stammered to Jacques that she would not leave immediately and that I should give her a few days. She continued: "I'm sure you can't force me to leave right now; give me a little more time." Upon his return, Jacques suggested to me, "Let's take a walk. I'll take you to eat at a restaurant."

Before heading to the restaurant, we stopped near the pier by the sea and stayed in the car to talk. He revealed to me what the young girl had asked of him. I responded with this remark: "You know, I don't want to hear anything. I came to my home. I'm staying here; let her go back to her mother." And I added: "I've let things happen my whole life, but never again will I let it happen." I continued: "It's stronger than me. I've suffered enough; I don't want to suffer anymore." I spoke firmly. I went on: "Jacques, too bad for her, because you haven't given me a chance for far too long!" Jacques stared at me without replying. In the end, he repeated his offer: "Enice, you haven't eaten anything since this morning. I need to take you to eat something, or you'll collapse." He concluded: "You need to have strength for what is going to happen tonight at my place."

Upon our return to his home, Jacques went upstairs to see the young girl to tell her that she had to leave that very evening. She cried, even threatening to kill herself. I advised Jacques to let her stay the night; she would leave early the next morning.

Jacques and I stayed on the lower floor. He took the opportunity to do some laundry. Then we worked on the computer. Jacques had every comfort at home: oven, refrigerator, freezer, fan nothing was missing in the house. Since it was equipped with an alternative system for when there was no electricity, everything continued to function. He was fully equipped: shower, toilet, etc. It was almost luxurious. And I, during all that time, was living in misery in Miragoâne because I had no comforts. I couldn't even wash myself, since there was no water.

I return to this story of the sleepless night. The young girl spent the night crying. She complained about what would happen to her, since she had nothing to live on or to eat.

We spent the night watching over her as one would a baby. I suggested to Jacques that he go see her from time to time throughout the night. I also proposed this idea: "Since she is miserable and poor, when she leaves, we will give her some money, and likewise every month, so she can live and return to school." Jacques agreed with me, but things did not go as we had hoped.

In the morning, at 6 o'clock, I told Jacques that it was time.

"She must leave, because we also need to sleep." He went upstairs to warn her to leave the house. Five minutes passed, and he hadn't come back down. I went up and told the young girl, "My little girl, get up, it's time for you to go. At this hour, you should be at school or at your mother's. You have no profession; you come to live with a married man so that he can take care of you. And your mother in all this what does she think?" I gave her a little lecture. She became gentle and apologized. She begged me not to abandon her, insisting that she needed me. A minute later, she was packing her bag. Jacques remained frozen, observing the young girl's reaction. During our conversation, I did not shout. I was calm with her, despite the fact that I had not slept for two nights.

Everything was going very well until we heard a knock. It was the young girl's mother, accompanied by her sister.

Jacques went downstairs to meet them. She started spouting nonsense. They were people deprived of everything; the mother demanded money to compensate her daughter. Jacques gave them money, a bicycle, and other items. They left. The young girl was still upstairs. But ten minutes later, the mother and her sister returned, claiming that the money Jacques had given them was not enough. They went into the store and seized a large amount of merchandise. They behaved like predators. Among other things, they even took a Preston microwave, dishes, food, and many other household items. When the young girl came downstairs, she, in turn, grabbed everything she could take, like a thief. Jacques and I watched them do it without saying a word. Then they left together, and we locked the door. They had managed to take the equivalent of more than $2,000.

We went upstairs to change the sheets and the pillows. I disinfected the room, and we went to bed. It was 11 a.m., but we couldn't sleep because of everything we had just seen and experienced. I had never met such people in my life, people so plundering. Their behavior broke my heart.

I later expressed these thoughts to Jacques: "How could you take advantage of miserable people to take such a young girl from her mother? While thinking that you didn't need her, that she was just there to satisfy your own interest, you used her." He responded with these words: "This is how it is here, Enice; we use the little ones for our needs." He admitted: "In a little while, you'll see that in Haiti, it will be a jungle, everyone for themselves. You must not pity others. Because those who are with you today will receive more from someone else tomorrow, and they will betray you without mercy! That's how it is here!"

Despite his explanations, I didn't understand anything he had just told me. I replied, however: "I hope you've learned your lesson." He didn't answer.

We were too tense to sleep, so we had to take some sedatives. Even so, I couldn't manage to sleep. I thought about everything I had just done and faced. I wondered if it was worth coming here to live with Jacques, alone, far from my family in Haiti and my family in Montreal. I was extremely sad. I hadn't revealed any of my doubts to Jacques. I was alone with him. He had a maid, but he had just let her go because she was related to the young girl.

I was the only one preparing the meals. Jacques, for his part, took care of the house. One fine day, two of his nephews came to visit us. They told me they had been Jacques's employees before the young girl arrived. I offered one of them the chance to come back to work for us, and I would pay him, but he would sleep at his own home. He left happy. With a decent salary, my proposal pleased him, and he left in good spirits.

I felt relieved of a burden. For three days, Jacques had closed the shop, intending to put it in order. Daniel, the rehired nephew, had, in the meantime, brought from the countryside one of his little brothers, aged 10. He would live with us as a servant without pay. His name was Roger. From that moment, the household was complete.

I was determined to do my best to make everything work well. I told Jacques: "We must trust each other and be willing to discuss things when they are not going well." I added: "Respect is very important in a couple." I continued: "I am sure that, if you also make an effort, everything will go well and we will be able to live together without major problems."

On this subject, everything was very clear in my mind. But the most important question for me concerned the writing of my memoirs. Since my return to Haiti, I had not written a single word about it. At the same time, I was determined to live in peace with my husband.

Present Moment

For the past few days, I have been struggling to resume my writing activity. I feel mentally and physically exhausted: my back, my legs, and my right hand are causing me intense pain. Despite my exercises, the blood does not circulate well in one of my legs. I have become very fragile and sensitive; I cry over nothing, yet I still make serious efforts to achieve my goal. There are passages that, once written, plunge me into a feeling of disgust. I could take a break for at least a day or two before continuing, but I will not give up I must hold on.

Part Two

A Presentation of Les Cayes

I will describe the little I know about Les Cayes while recounting my stay in this city.

Our House

The house was located on Second Grand Street (called Rue General Bauvoir). One of Jacques' cousins owned a large property on this street. It was divided into two twin two-story houses, with a large shared garage.

Each family had access to services specific to them. The only amenities we shared were the water from the cisterns and the septic tanks. Jacques occupied the smaller house; he had signed a one-year lease.

In truth, it was the lower part of a hall, converted into a house. There was a gallery on the right side, with the entrance to the shared garage. The shop was located at the front of the house. Immediately after that was the dining room and the kitchen, with a door and a window opening onto the garage, as well as the toilets at the back with a shower and a bathtub. In the dining room, Jacques had arranged a room for the maid and the little servant.

From the garage, one could go to the back of the house and up to the roof to hang laundry. We did not have a yard. We could only see the sun through the large front door that opened onto the gallery.

On the upper floor were the living room, a small office, and a storage room. At the back, Jacques had installed a partition to create a closed bedroom. A staircase led to a locked door that no one could cross without Jacques knowing. He had installed an alarm system on this door. The upper floor did not have a window overlooking the garage, but the house had a large balcony overlooking the shop. Since the upper wall of the shop was made of concrete blocks with small openings between the bricks, one could see everything happening outside and inside the shop. However, there was not much air or light; the sun did not penetrate. To remedy this, Jacques had placed fans and electric lights throughout the house.

Sometimes, when I felt short of air, I would go for a walk on the gallery, provided the almost constant dust was not completely unbearable. The employees were always dusting the merchandise and furniture. As for me, I spent the entire day cleaning my nostrils to remove this dust.

This, then, was the house where I lived with Jacques during my stay in Les Cayes.

Part Three

My Beginnings in Les Cayes, January 1999

Over the days, I gradually became familiar with the house. First, Jacques had taken me to pick up my suitcases from my sister in Miragoâne. We stayed there for two days. We also took the opportunity to have the land surveyed.

I was completely confused. Jacques was in a hurry to settle the property division. He told me it was better to resolve this matter quickly so that everything could be sold. I replied that I didn't want to rush anything, especially since he had the money needed to support us in the meantime. He shouted at me: "I can't move from one city to another at all times over a land division issue!" I insisted that he tell me how much money he had left. He urged me not to worry and promised I would know soon. Wanting not to bother him further on this topic, I never mentioned it again. Once the land surveying was finished, we returned to Les Cayes. We gave our phone number to the surveyor so he could inform us when the documents were ready.

Everything was going well at the house. I became familiar with the little servant, Roger, and the young employee, Daniel. This nephew of Jacques helped him from time to time to repair the car and the van. He had a brother, Tome, and their cousin Jacob, who was also Jacques' nephew. They would come to pick up Daniel almost every evening and would take the opportunity to have their only meal of the day, which I had set aside for them. I soon realized that these young boys had no other family ties, no money, and no place to sleep. They were not attending school either. I offered to help them if they decided to enroll in at least evening classes. We gave them money for the registration, but they spent it on other things.

Jacques then scolded me: "I warned you that these young ones are not serious; they are used to their miseries." I partly agreed with him, but

I still believed we should lend them a hand. So I continued to feed and clothe them. As for the nephew Daniel, he received his salary each month and was treated very well. The little servant, Roger, was also treated very well. When he arrived, he was thin, with protruding ears and eyes, hollow temples, a big belly, and legs like sticks. Just a week later, he had gained weight. I bought him nice clothes and shoes. He ate and slept well. He was always clean. I loved him very much.

Little Roger could neither read nor write. Before enrolling him in school, I gave him lessons in reading and writing. After two months, I registered him in a school not far from our house, where he attended half a day every day. He respected me and obeyed me obediently; he was my little guardian. He watched over everything that happened in the house and the shop. One day, I lost sight of this little boy. I do not know what became of him. I would have loved to continue helping him. He had told me about his life of poverty while living with his parents and siblings. He confided that, to stave off hunger, they drank water and ate papaya leaves. In the evening, they went to bed very early and woke up very late. This routine helped them avoid being hungry for too long.

In their village, when an animal died, they did not worry about why. They hurried to take a piece of the meat and kept it to eat over the week, even if it had begun to rot. His two older brothers were as thin as he was when they arrived at my house. During my stay in Les Cayes, I did everything I could to assist them, to give them some comfort and a little happiness. I felt great sorrow seeing people live in such misery. I shared what I could with them, and I do not regret it at all.

In any case, I do not hesitate to affirm that if I am still on this earth, it is thanks to the poor people who brought a little happiness into my life while I was living in Les Cayes and Miragoâne.

At the beginning, Jacques took me on a tour of the city so I could get accustomed to it. He showed me the place where he got drinking water, from an artesian well. He took me to the Les Cayes pier. We often ate at restaurants. Sometimes, on weekends, we organized picnics with the young people. We would spend the day at Gelée Beach.

January 24, 1999

It was Sunday of my second week since arriving in Les Cayes. We went to Gelée Beach with the four boys. We had a barbecue, and the boys could not hide their joy. It was the first time they had seen and eaten meat cooked over charcoal. Their happiness truly delighted me. Jacques, on his part, was resting. The wind was strong, so I did not swim. I strolled peacefully along the beach, feeling the warm sand beneath my feet. This sensation brought me great comfort. I looked out over the expanse of the ocean and its waves. I felt a delightful joy. At the same time, I reflected on everything I had experienced before. I thanked God and thought of my children and grandchildren in Canada. I knew they were well. I concluded that now it was my turn to experience a little happiness.

During a conversation with Jacques, I warned him that it was time to stop foolishness and that we needed to commit to living in harmony. I was his legitimate wife, and respect had to prevail between us.

It was truly my goal to do everything possible to ensure things went well between Jacques and me. I anticipated that I would have to sacrifice my comfortable life, to be away from my children and grandchildren, and to return to live in a country where I no longer knew anyone. Because of him, I was at odds with my sister Irène, whom I love so much, as well as with my sister in Miragoâne. For all these reasons, I had to succeed at any cost.

At first, for at least three weeks, there was harmony and joy, but I suspected that Jacques surely had some ulterior motive. At the same time, I no longer understood myself. I had become less sentimental. I felt as though I was not really at home. My spontaneity had almost disappeared, but I did everything I could to ensure Jacques suspected nothing. I felt betrayed. On his side, he became increasingly secretive. And I no longer believed in his sincerity. I was certain that, as usual, he was hiding something from me.

Over the days, Jacques had developed the bad habit of leaving the house early in the afternoon. He always left at the same time, around 2:30 p.m., and returned around 6:30 p.m. He always invented an excuse. At those moments, I felt alone, and the reality of my situation saddened me. He was surely doing it on purpose to annoy me. One evening, he returned at 9 p.m.; I could hardly believe it. This time, I did not accept it, especially since he had promised to go out with me that evening. I found myself in a city where I knew no one, and I expected him to be more understanding. He should have realized that when he left, I felt extremely lonely. Moreover, anything could happen during his absence.

Every time he returned home, he overwhelmed me with negative words. He spouted nonsense and spoke about my ex-husband and his own adventures with women. His behavior toward me seemed completely irrational.

I had believed that this stay in Haiti would bring me peace, but I refused to admit that my dreams were far from coming true. In fact, the problems were just beginning. Jacques looked for every opportunity to hurt me. I then reasoned with myself: "It's really too late to go back, and in any case, it would be very shameful for me if I left. So, I'm here, and I stay, that's all." I concluded: "In any case, he is destroying himself." All in all, I felt at peace with myself. But he was disturbed, like a person harboring a demon in his heart. At one point, he even threatened to hit me. I defended myself. I warned him to change his behavior because I could become dangerous if pushed, especially since I had never personally harmed him.

Day by day, I realized that happiness would not come on its own. I would have to build my own happiness. Gradually, I began to take my place in this unfamiliar city. Jacques' cousin, Zita, arrived from

Montreal for a stay with her brother. She brought me news of my children. My daughter, Natatsha, sent me photos of my grandchildren, and I was thrilled to see them.

I immediately called Natatsha to thank her; she had been expecting my call anyway. She confided that life in Montreal was difficult for her because she had fallen ill and could not work. After paying her rent, the little money she had left was not enough to buy food. The children were not eating enough. I authorized her to withdraw from my bank account each month to help remedy the situation.

It angered me to learn that my own children were going hungry in Montreal while, in my house in Les Cayes, the children ate their fill and wasted food in my absence. I constantly scolded them about the fact that their brother and sister had nothing to eat in the countryside. I also called my son Max, who told me that everything was fine on his side. He and his wife were expecting a baby in September. I was relieved to finally hear some good news.

It was now the beginning of February. I hardly went out. Jacques did not take me anywhere. I went to church every Sunday afternoon. I was bored. I was staying in a hot country, and he knew how much I loved the sea. Yet he no longer took me to the beach, always promising it would be "next time."

One weekend, my friend Nelia from Miragoâne and her husband Stone came to see us. They were on their way to Dame Marie, a town two hours from Les Cayes. They invited us to join them for the day. I was very interested in the offer, sure that Jacques would agree. He told them that we would meet them the next day and that they could count on our presence. When they left, he said to me: "Don't think I'm going there; take that idea out of your head. I won't go, and neither will you, because you don't know the place. So forget it." Although I insisted, he did not change his mind. I was truly disappointed because I wanted to see something different, which would have done me good.

I remember that on February 14, 1999, Valentine's Day, it had been one month since I had resumed married life with Jacques. I had planned to spend a quiet, pleasant evening in his company. That evening, I had described in my journal.

February 14, 1999 Journal

That evening, after having a quiet dinner, I took my shower. Jacques, too, was ready to take his. Then, there was a knock at the door. Roger went to answer it. It was a boy who wanted to speak to Jacques. He informed him that the girl required his presence; she needed him. I told him to let this troublesome girl know that he was busy. He did not listen and went to meet her.

I decided to go up to my room. I was very furious. When Jacques returned, I told him that I was not at all happy with the way he was acting. Instead of apologizing, he reacted by spouting nonsense. Out of anger, I broke a pot. He hit me, and we fought all because of that opportunistic girl. This incident made me sick. But after two days, Jacques and I reconciled.

Our arguments always ended in sex carried out with violence. It was disgusting. I had noticed that whenever he wanted violent sex, he always arranged a problem so that we would argue first.

I continue my story

Over the days, Jacques became calmer. He went out less often than before. I managed to hire a maid, Maguy. She was small in stature and knew a little reading and writing. I could make her a grocery list so that she could buy the necessary items. She was Baptist. I gave her Saturdays off so that she could attend church. She had a three-year-old child, whom she had left in the countryside under the care of her mother. Every two weeks, she was allowed to visit her son and bring food and supplies to her mother. All the employees were well treated.

I considered them as members of the family, especially since I knew no one in this unfamiliar town. At least I could count on them.

At one point, the surveyor called us to inform that the documents regarding the land division were ready. We decided to return to Miragoâne to meet the notary and potential buyers. Jacques insisted that I sell the lands. He tried to convince me that with that money, I would become financially independent. After some hesitation, I finally listened to him.

Upon arriving in Miragoâne, I went to see my sister Claire, where I intended to stay this time. She and her husband were not happy to see me, and they made that clear. I did not stay long; their reception made me sad. We then went to my friend Nelia's house; from there, we contacted the notary, who asked us to meet him with the surveyor on one of the plots, as there were interested buyers.

After verifying that the documents were in proper order, I paid him what remained owed. That same afternoon, we managed to sell one of the plots. The next day, we finalized the papers. Back in Les Cayes, I returned the $2,000 that Jacques had lent me for the various transactions. He told me that he no longer had money to pay for the house and electricity. He also planned to repair his van and cover other expenses. I asked why he had not paid the rent. He explained that the payment was a year overdue, that his account in Haiti was empty, and that the rest of his money was in an account in Montreal. My only reaction was to give him the bulk of the money from the sale of the first plot.

This story of selling the plots had become very stressful for me. On one side was Jacques, pressuring me to sell, and on the other was my sister Claire, pleading with me not to sell the land. I was exhausted by all these discussions; it felt as if I were constantly soliciting favors. The pressure Jacques exerted was almost unbearable. In truth, I did not need the money to live it was he who needed it, and he seemed willing to do anything to obtain it.

Since I wanted to free myself from all this stress and no longer deal with the land sale, Jacques suggested that I grant him a notarized power of attorney for the matter. I agreed, in order to avoid any confrontation with my sister. I deposited the little money that remained in the bank as a simple precaution. Later, I sent the documents regarding the land division to all my brothers and sisters, so that everyone concerned would know what was rightfully theirs.

Meanwhile, I had not resumed writing, which made me very anxious. My life with Jacques was like a roller coaster, to the point that I could not find the peace needed to write my memoirs. It was crucial that I do something, but I did not yet know what.

One day, I decided to pick up my journal again, but I could no longer find it. I was unhappy. I believed that Jacques had torn it up. For two months, I resigned myself to writing on loose sheets of paper. In the meantime, a painful sorrow gnawed at my heart because of the loss of my journal.

Part Four

Change in Jacques's Behavior

Since our return from Miragoâne, Jacques had become silent. He hardly spoke to me, and I had no one to confide in. So, I immersed myself in reading. I was no longer writing; I didn't have the headspace for it. Jacques was constantly glued to his computer. On my side, I felt deeply unhappy. I missed my family in Montreal. I had no friends in Les Cayes. Jacques, on the other hand, declared himself very comfortable in this city. He had his nephews, his cousin, and, as he once told me: *"Here in Haiti, I'm on my territory; I can do what I want, and also what I want with you. I take orders from no one!"*

Then the following idea came to me: I would buy a ticket to Montreal, where I would stay for two months. I would spend Easter there with my children, and who knows, maybe I would stay. I shared my travel plans with Jacques. He confided that he was entertaining the same idea. We went up to Port-au-Prince to purchase tickets and make the reservations. The departure was set for March 10, 1999.

Upon our return to Les Cayes, we spent a week preparing our luggage and securing the house. Jacques did not want to leave his nephews at home for fear of thieves. We sent the young servant, Roger, to his parents, giving him provisions and money.

I was eager to leave. It had been three months since I had seen my children and grandchildren. I couldn't wait to see them again. I called my children to let them know that we would arrive in Montreal on March 10. They awaited us joyfully.

Chapter 9

Easter in Montreal

Part One

My Stay in Montreal, Easter 1999

Upon our return to Montreal, the children were happy to see me again. But a coldness had set in between them and Jacques. They were on the defensive. They did not trust him, which, all things considered, was understandable. We had stayed at Natatsha's place, who had lent us her bedroom. However, this arrangement made me genuinely uncomfortable. I told Jacques that we needed to rent an apartment for the two months we would be staying in Montreal.

I retrieved the furniture I had stored before leaving for Haiti. We were able to find an unfurnished apartment, which we rented for two months. I had a telephone installed. I then demanded from Jacques concrete proof of the remaining amount in his bank account. Every day, he claimed there was no urgency in checking it, and each time, he found a new excuse.

During this stay in Montreal, we were able to visit our doctors and renew prescriptions. With the money I had, we purchased goods destined for Haiti. These were shipped by container, along with the rest of my furniture.

We returned to Haiti on May 3. I believe I had wonderful moments with my children and grandchildren, and enjoyed a pleasant Easter. I had visited my sister and brother several times. Irène showed indifference toward me, while my brother Robert's health worried me greatly.

I eventually learned that Jacques no longer had any money. For a long time, he had been telling me stories that no longer held up. It was only a few months after our return to Haiti that he admitted he had thoroughly enjoyed spending that money. He had recklessly indulged with his mistress in Toronto and the young girl in Haiti! In six months, he had spent more than $100,000 the amount he had obtained following his accident. During our stay in Montreal, he had secretly sent money to the young Haitian girl. I discovered this thanks to a receipt. He could no longer deny it.

Clearly, he had not been sincere with me at all. He was hiding far too many facts.

Part Two

My Return to Haiti and Les Cayes

May 1999

Upon returning to Haiti, I decided to change my behavior and focus more on myself. I set the goal of finishing my book at all costs, of writing my memoirs without fail. It was the month of May, but I had still delayed starting the project.

I resolved to ignore all the obstacles Jacques might create, in order to channel my energy effectively. I had noticed, for example, that he seemed to pay attention every time I resumed writing. He constantly sought ways to distract me. I prayed that he would eventually leave me alone. One day, I found my journal on my desk it was as if a miraculous hand had placed it there. Truly mysterious! Had it been lost?

From that moment on, my distrust grew. I was deeply troubled learning how Jacques had spent his money. I even wondered if he had come to fetch me from Montreal because he no longer had funds. He knew that my parents had left me part of their inheritance. Yet I had always told him I would not touch it. This time, he once again set a trap for me and I fell into it. He usually waited until I was in a vulnerable moment to catch me in his snares. I had become his puppet, and I invariably took the bait.

Part Three

Jacques Changes His Attitude

Since our return to Haiti, both Jacques and I had changed considerably. During the day, he repaired cars in the garage; in the afternoon, he would go out and return late in the evening. He would settle at his computer, and when bedtime came, he would take a shower and fall asleep immediately afterward.

I had the impression that he was trying to evade me. I observed him silently. At the same time, I devoted myself to my book. I had a lot of free time since his nephew and little Roger took care of the shop. The maid, for her part, looked after the house. Nevertheless, I trusted no one except the little boy. Ever since Jacques' nephew, Daniel, had given me contaminated water, I no longer believed in their loyalty. I had spent an entire week suffering from diarrhea and stomach pains.

Jacques had resumed seeing the young Haitian girl and maintained ongoing contact with the girl in Toronto. Whenever I tried to speak to him about it, he became angry. He constantly found excuses, claiming that his financial support for the young girl was simply because she had nothing to eat. On the surface, the argument seemed valid, but it did not explain why he saw her so frequently.

Over time, however, the situation improved somewhat. On Sundays, for example, we would go together to church, to the Gelée beach, or to restaurants. Nevertheless, I remained cautious. I had become friends with the manager of a store selling construction materials, located near our house.

She would visit me at the shop almost every day. We discussed everything. I felt less alone. She invited me to her home and offered advice on how to behave with the people of Les Cayes. Gradually, the locals began to show me respect, though I still remained careful.

Part Four

Journal on Mother's Day

It is May 28, 1999, the day before Mother's Day in Haiti. My memories take me back to my youth, to the death of my mother, and the overwhelming grief I experienced at that time. It is truly difficult for me to describe this period of my childhood the process awakens a very deep sorrow within me. I even cry, yet I must continue if I want to complete the writing of my memoirs. On the other hand, with each new passage I write, I feel as though I am freeing myself from one of my ghosts.

Part Five

Mother's Day in Haiti

May 30, 1999   Journal

Today is Mother's Day in Haiti. I thought of my children. My husband Jacques woke me up this morning with joy to say, "Happy Mother's Day." I was genuinely surprised because since we got married, he had never done that. His gesture gave me great pleasure. I pretended to thank him, but he left shortly afterward, telling me he had a very important appointment. I did not stop him, though I found his behavior a little suspicious. I quickly pushed the negative thought aside; I did not want to ruin my day. Fortunately, the day went well.

I thought a lot about my past life, my mother, and also my sisters and brothers, whose behavior toward me had changed significantly since the land division. Life is strange. Yet each of them had received their share.

On the evening of May 30, Jacques and I went to church and then to a restaurant for dinner. He mentioned that he would have liked to take me to the cinema, but unfortunately, there was no movie theater in Les Cayes.

If I reflected on my past that day, it was because I could not understand my siblings' reactions toward me. At the same time, I felt it might have been to protect me from Jacques. They had probably guessed things that I had not suspected. I was blind, like a sleepwalker, noticing nothing in Jacques's schemes. I understood absolutely nothing. I reacted like a zombie who obeyed him to the letter.

Part Six

My Pastime in Les Cayes

It was June. I was able to speak with my daughter on June 2, 1999. She gave me updates about the family. My little granddaughter, Elle-Camay, had just undergone a tonsil operation, and everything had gone well. She had also secured a contract for a film production. All these good news reassured me.

Daily life in Les Cayes was going more or less smoothly. Many people, especially young people, came to see me to ask for advice on one matter or another for instance, on travel arrangements, administrative matters, etc. I went out very little, except to attend church on Sunday afternoons and to accompany Jacques every other day to fetch water from the well. I loved this spot because it was tucked away from the main city.

At the entrance stood a large, old two-story house, uninhabited. The well was located at the back of the large courtyard, near a stream. The area was surrounded by gardens with large trees, mango trees, avocado trees, breadfruit trees, rice fields, small millet plots, and so on. You could hear the cries of birds, the rustling of leaves, and echoes whose resonance produced a soft, enchanting music one could never have imagined. I don't know if others perceived it, but I did! I was happy; the effect was beautiful and gentle. I loved going there. I felt calm and eager to continue.

Sometimes I derived immense pleasure simply from watching passersby: the market women carrying heavy bundles on their heads; the servants going to the market to prepare meals; the students heading to or returning from school. Loafers lingered all day, merely watching flies fly or dozing off, or criticizing or praising people. Men ogled the young girls' buttocks and breasts.

I remember that across from our house, there were two two-story stores. The occupants lived on the upper floors. The lower floors were actually halls whose doors were always closed. Instead of walking in the street, passersby used the galleries to protect themselves from the sun and avoid stepping on the crushed stones that made up the streets. At a seemingly designated spot, whenever someone man or woman felt an urgent need to urinate, they would relieve themselves without any embarrassment. And the dogs naturally imitated the humans. It was really amusing to watch.

I loved those moments when market women came to sell me products from their gardens fruits and vegetables. They took their time. One or another would say: "Madam, I enjoy coming to sell you my products. You appreciate all humans; you speak to us. And you always give us something to drink. You take a little time to listen to us talk about our little problems and miseries." Before leaving, these vendors would always assure me that God would bless me.

All these people respected me, and I treated them the same way. They were people like you and me, but with a different upbringing, lifestyle, and social conditions. They did not expect much from us just a little attention to relieve their miseries and problems. I went to live there without knowing what I would do. In the end, I managed to help many people who sought my advice and experience.

I do not recount these facts to boast. I only want to note that, in retrospect, I do not at all regret having lived in this city and having assisted human beings in need.

Part Seven

My Travels Between Les Cayes, Miragoâne, and Port-au-Prince

Despite the fatigue caused by my back-and-forth trips between Les Cayes, Miragoâne, and Port-au-Prince, I truly enjoyed these moments. Even though the van broke down repeatedly, along with the inconveniences that came with it, I focused on appreciating nature, reading, writing, or observing people quarrel or have fun. In Haiti, there is always the chance to witness or hear comical scenes, so boredom is never an issue.

The city of Les Cayes is located in the south of the country, in the middle of a plain. However, the surrounding regions are mountainous, which I loved most during my travels. I enjoyed driving on the National Road leaving Les Cayes, listening to relaxing music in the car. One could admire the lush mountains on both sides of the road, dotted with gardens, trees, and a few small houses. A little further, approaching Mount Saint-Georges, you could see the ocean and the beach along the Saint-Louis–Aquin road from the summit. It was a marvelous view from the top of the mountain, giving me pure and gentle pleasure. During the trip, we would stop to buy provisions lemons, grapefruits, and vegetables for ourselves, but also for my sister Claire, my friend Nelia, and relatives living in Port-au-Prince.

Upon arriving at our land in Chalon, we would take a break while the gardener picked coconuts and mangoes for us. We stopped at Des Ruisseaux to eat at a small restaurant called "Chez Simone" (the restaurant of the blind; no meat), where the food was always good. The place was always filled with regulars who either boasted or played cards. I observed their behavior while Jacques joined in their conversations.

In Miragoâne, the downtown area was crowded with people of all kinds: merchants, buyers, servants, etc. Everyone spoke loudly. Vans and trucks circulated through streets that were too narrow for them. The heat was excessive. Merchants set up their items on the galleries and streets, and whenever a large truck arrived, they had to remove everything and put it back afterward. It was an indescribable hubbub! At the port, large ships were anchored, unloading merchandise.

All the noise was overwhelming, yet I sought it it gave me a sensation of life. However, I could not bear to hear this infernal noise every day or see my compatriots live this way like madmen. Who would have believed that 40 years earlier, this was a paradise city?

When traveling from Miragoâne to Port-au-Prince, the landscape changes. The journey is longer because the road is unpaved. Many sections are completely bumpy and full of large holes. The landscape is less mountainous between Miragoâne and Petit-Goâve. Along the road, you can see banana and coconut plantations, among other crops. Beyond Petit-Goâve lies Morne Tapion, formerly infamous, now paved. Morne Tapion and Morne Oranger on the Les Cayes route held the record for fatal accidents in southern Haiti on the National Road south. Once you descend Morne Tapion, the landscape opens into plains leading to Port-au-Prince, whose Carrefour district has an atmosphere reminiscent of Miragoâne.

Very frequently during these long trips, we had to repair two or three flat tires or other mechanical issues.

Despite these inconveniences, I enjoyed traveling because, during these moments, I was outside the house, seeing people and realities different from the everyday scene of dusty streets and cement houses in Les Cayes. I also felt less worried about my life. When staying in Port-au-Prince, I felt closer to my family in Canada. Phone communication was easier, and I was near the international airport in case of emergency.

This sums up my travels during these few months spent in Haiti. The experience was not perfect, but at least I had the opportunity to escape a little.

Part Eight

Jacques' Proposal

For several days, I had been struggling to write, unable to concentrate. I made several attempts, but they were all in vain, resulting in a significant delay in writing my book. This part of my life, which I had long planned to write about, was actually one of the happiest periods of my youth. I felt psychologically blocked.

In addition, I began to have problems with one of Jacques' nephews. He was causing trouble, threatening to leave, while shifting the blame onto his younger brother. He had grown jealous, believing that little Roger was being treated too well even though he received his weekly salary and was well-fed. I no longer trusted him after this incident. I felt unsafe around him. I had discussed this with Jacques, who suggested giving the nephew one final chance. If he didn't change his behavior, he would be dismissed.

One Sunday, Jacques and I went to relax at Gelée Beach. He knew I loved the beach and that the sea calmed me. It was June 13, 1999. I don't know what went through his mind or what his true plan was. He said to me: "Enice, what would you think if we built a house on the land you own in Chalon? That way, you could have your own home, be close to your family, and we could have our farm."

All sorts of ideas ran through my mind as I listened to his proposal, but I didn't answer him right away. His suggestion seemed reasonable: I would live peacefully in nature, the young girl would no longer bother me, I would be closer to Port-au-Prince to speak with my children or take a flight to Montreal whenever I felt blue. But at the same time, I imagined that Jacques would be freer to continue his sexual affair with the young girl from Les Cayes. I quickly dismissed this thought, concluding that I needed to think of myself first.

A few days later, I told him that I accepted the project, on the condition that I would supervise the construction with him. He agreed. He informed me that that very evening, we would start tracing the house's plan. He seemed kind and considerate toward me. Perhaps he was hiding his true intentions, but I calculated that at least I would not be spending all that money in vain.

The House Plan

We worked on sketches of the house plan until a very late hour at night. Then we agreed that we needed to go to the actual land to take precise measurements. The date set for this visit to Miragoâne was June 17, 1999.

It was already a beginning. From that evening, communication between Jacques and me became easier. He seemed more relaxed and attentive toward me. We spent a good week together. He showed me a lot of love and was more tender with me. He no longer went out every evening as he had before.

Part Nine

Measurements and Information Collected in Miragoâne

Upon our arrival at the site, we shared our project with the caretaker of the land. We then began taking measurements regarding the length and width of the main house, as well as those of the servants' quarters and the boys' dormitory, the kitchen, and the warehouse. We also measured a space where the caretaker would build his own small house. On the remaining part of the land, we planned to construct a large farm with a stable, because I love horses. My dream has always been to own a ranch one day. I have always been fascinated by horses. When I am in the presence of a horse, I feel safe; at the same time, I feel a gentle inner peace.

In Montreal, every year, my son and his wife Yole would take me to a ranch. My daughter-in-law rides horses herself, but I would pet these graceful animals and watch them walk and gallop. At the same time, I would help my grandchildren ride by holding the reins and guiding the horses as they trotted.

I continue my account on the Chalon property

We stayed the whole day on the land. This contact with nature did me a lot of good. I went to visit my sister and her husband and shared with them my decision to build. They congratulated me on it, but remained wary of Jacques. I had a feeling that my sister Claire wanted to speak to me. I could guess it in her eyes. I almost heard her warning me: "Nounoune, be careful, don't trust him." But I didn't want to listen. I felt lost, refusing to hear or see.

I then went to my friend Nelia's house. She was happy to hear the news about the construction project. She offered us a place to stay on the nights we would come to Miragoâne to oversee the work. Since it was late, she invited us to sleep there that night. The next day, June 19, we returned to Les Cayes.

Here is what I wrote that day.

June 19, 1999

This morning, we returned very early from Miragoâne. We picked up the boys to bring them back home. After dropping them off, Jacques claimed he was going out to run some errands. By chance, I stepped out onto the porch and saw him park his car in front of the young girl's house. She came out to talk to him, and he gave her something. When she noticed me, she gave a proud little smirk while looking at me mockingly. I pretended not to notice and went back inside.

If only Jacques knew how much it hurt me for him to act that way! Only I know the depth of my suffering. And most of all, I kept it all in my heart. The way he responded when I spoke to him about the incident he made a huge scene. After everything I had done for him, he should have shown me some respect. He even insisted that he hadn't noticed my presence on the porch and that, in any case, it was nothing just that the young girl had asked for a little money.

Following this dispute

I no longer wanted to build. Then I thought it might be better this way; perhaps we would find the solution to all these problems.

It was June 24, the Feast of Saint John the Baptist, the patron saint of the people of Miragoâne. I did not go to Miragoâne for the event, but I prayed to Saint John the Baptist for my family in Montreal and my friends in Miragoâne. I also thought of those who had passed away. I took advantage of the rest of the day to write about a part of my past my life with the nuns in Miragoâne. I felt happy writing this part of my life. I did not want the story to end; I lingered on it. I felt good.

Towards the end of June, more precisely on the 29th, we went back to Port-au-Prince with all the boys because Jacques had to settle an electricity contract for the house in Laboule. He was also expecting a delivery of merchandise, as well as the rest of my belongings, coming from Montreal. I was happy to go to the capital because I love that environment. I enjoy it very much there. I can write in peace outside, comfortably seated under the mango trees.

This trip in Haiti was an adventure and a discovery for me. I love adventures, and I love to dream. So, I was always in full action. Over time, I noticed that I always fall unexpectedly into events that give me strong emotions every time I risk the unknown!

Part Ten

The La Boule Neighborhood in Port-au-Prince

My Journal

June 29, 1999   Journal

I arrived in Port-au-Prince yesterday with Jacques, his nephew, and little Roger. Jacques needs to redo the electricity in the house at La Boule. It's a very large house. The interior makes me think of the house I have always dreamed of. It feels good to be here. For the moment, I am settling on the terrace to write. The weather is beautiful, and the sky is blue. The house is perched on the mountain. I can breathe freely. I don't feel like I'm in Port-au-Prince. It's so beautiful. There are many trees around, and large houses. I'm happy to be here. I don't know how long we will stay, but in any case, I will take advantage of the time to write part of my book and breathe the fresh air.

I continue my story.

During my stay at La Boule, I thought of nothing else but writing my memoirs. Every morning after breakfast, I would sit outside on one of the terrace steps, under a mango tree, to write. I always began with my morning prayer, after which I got to work. I took a break at noon for lunch and resumed around 2:00 p.m., continuing until 5:30 p.m. Between writing sessions, I walked a few minutes to stretch my legs and oxygenate my brain.

I paid no attention to Jacques. The young ones knew they had to prepare the meals and assist Jacques. I was not part of their world. When I wrote, I was elsewhere, in the past. On some days, I visited family in Port-au-Prince. We bought materials and did grocery shopping with Jacques. We stayed two weeks at La Boule. Around

July 15, we returned to Les Cayes with the merchandise and furniture that had arrived from Montreal.

For a few days, everything went almost smoothly with Jacques. He went out less often. It should be noted that we took care of selling the received merchandise in order to begin construction of the house. We were also concerned with selling my lands.

I continue my story

For two days, I completely ignored Jacques. I felt disgust toward him. I devoted myself to writing and reading. On his side, he tried to be kind to me and did not go out. Eventually, I spoke to him. He told me that I should not worry about this matter with the young girl; if he had given her money, it was so that she would not harm him or hurt me. He was acting this way to protect me. We reconciled. I agreed to make love with him.

The next day, on the 24th, a little girl came to our door; she wanted to see Jacques. His young mistress wanted him to send her water. But this time, I did not accept it. I immediately shouted to Jacques: "I think you have no choice but to go live with her, because I can no longer live with you here. After all, I am going to be with my children." He insisted that the young girl had acted deliberately to provoke us, both him and me. He said we had to avoid falling into her trap at all costs. He promised me that we would go to Miragoâne the following week to start building the house. That way, she would be forced to leave us alone!

Jacques needed me. Without me, the house could not be built, since he no longer had any money. The project could only be completed with the proceeds from the sale of the land. To keep me, I demanded that he completely change his behavior. Respect on his part was no longer negotiable, I finally told him.

Chapter 10

Construction of the House in Haiti

Part One

Starting Construction of the House in Chalon

On Sunday, August 1, 1999, we closed the house and left for a week in Miragoâne to begin the construction work. We brought tools, a generator, and a concrete mixer that we had purchased in Port-au-Prince, as well as a trailer to transport accessories, rebar, and cement. I had also prepared notebooks, accounting and payroll sheets, and schedules. Everything was well planned and organized. This time, we took little Roger along with the two young boys. They could lend us a hand. To complete the workforce, we also hired local workers.

On Monday, August 2, 1999, we first took measurements for the foundations, after which we began digging them. Since no water line was available, Jacques made all the necessary arrangements to ensure that the site and its surroundings had access to water. These operations took the entire day. The neighbors praised Jacques greatly for his efforts.

Work continued eight hours a day, Monday to Friday, until noon. The workers, fed on site, were paid by the hour. On Friday at noon, after distributing the workers' wages and storing materials and tools at my friend Nélia's place, we returned home to Les Cayes. This left only two days for cleaning, laundry, and other tasks before leaving again very early the following Monday or Tuesday morning.

In this way, construction progressed well. Within three weeks, we had dug the foundations, poured concrete, placed the metal equipment for the columns, and so on. The next step was laying the blocks. We had already dug the septic tank.

I had very little time left to write, but it was on my mind almost constantly.

Here is what I wrote in my journal during that time.

August 21, 1999 Journal

Today is August 21, 1999. I haven't written for two weeks because of the time devoted to construction.

Today, Addedy, the daughter of Aunt Dédia, is getting married in New York. I am thinking a lot about her. I had asked my daughter to go on my behalf. I must return to Montreal on September 17, and then I will visit them in New York upon arrival.

I must finish my book; I need to resume writing if I want to complete it by September. I am taking advantage of this afternoon to continue working on it.

August 24, 1999 Journal

I spoke with Natatsha this morning on the phone. She told me she had just returned from New York following Addedy's wedding. She seemed pleased. We didn't talk for long. I feel sad today; I am thinking about the children, the wedding, and the whole family, but it's alright I resign myself. My heart feels heavy because, despite all the sacrifices I have made, I have a strong feeling that Jacques and the young girl are plotting something together. I am sure I will find out eventually, thanks to God.

I say nothing; I let him act. In the meantime, I try to guess what he has in mind. For my part, I have a clear goal, and I must achieve it.

We spent the end of August and the beginning of September shuttling between Miragoâne and Les Cayes for the construction. I was exhausted and eager to return to Montreal around September 3. We went to Port-au-Prince to make a reservation for departure on

September 17, 1999. I visited my brother Alain, who had recently returned to live in Haiti. He told me that my sister Irène had informed him that my brother Robert was ill in Montreal. The news deeply troubled me; I care for my little brother very much and consider him a friend. I didn't know why I had been having trouble sleeping for the past few days I was feeling his illness without realizing it yet. This information confirmed my plan to travel to Montreal.

In the meantime, I was neglecting the writing of my book. I couldn't concentrate; the construction had completely exhausted me. I finally accepted that I would not be able to finish the book before my departure to Montreal.

We spent four days in Port-au-Prince. At the time of our departure for Les Cayes on September 6, 1999, I received some good news from my daughter. I recorded it in my journal. Here is what I wrote in that circumstance.

September 7, 1999 Journal

Yesterday morning, September 6, I was still in Port-au-Prince. The idea came to me to call my daughter Natatsha to inform her of our arrival in Montreal on September 17. That's when she shared the wonderful news: the birth of Max and Yole's child, a little boy. He was born on September 5 at 10 a.m. I was overjoyed by this news. I felt Max's joy as well. I couldn't wait to be there to see this little six-pound bundle. It was wonderful. I was a grandmother for the third time. I thanked God for this blessing.

Part Two

Preparing Our Bags

We returned to Les Cayes to pack our bags, close up the house, and remind the caretaker to carefully watch over the materials on the property.

Around September 14, we went up to Port-au-Prince to catch our flight to Montreal. I had never been so eager to leave, and for many reasons: to see my grandson and his family, to visit my daughter and her children, my sister and brother, to consult my doctor about my health, and to rest. My disappointment at not having finished my book was great, but I was determined to complete it.

Three days before our departure for Canada, I developed rather severe diarrhea and felt very weak. I was eager to be in Montreal with my loved ones. We took the plane on September 17, 1999. This time, it was for a stay of three weeks, no more.

Part Three

A Short Stay in Montreal and Return to Haiti

Upon my arrival in Montreal, I was even sicker. I was still suffering from diarrhea, to the point that the next morning I could barely walk. I went to the nearest clinic, where the doctor on duty prescribed medication that helped me greatly. Two days later, I was feeling fully recovered. After my brief stay in Montreal, here is what I wrote in my journal upon returning to Haiti.

My Stay in Montreal

October 15, 1999   Journal

It is 5 p.m., and I am sitting on a chair in our shop in Les Cayes. I returned from Montreal three days ago. We had spent nearly a month there. The children were happy to see us. I was also delighted to be reunited with my little family. I held my son Max's baby boy in my arms a beautiful little child. Max seemed to have drawn him himself; he was so perfect. I blessed him and thanked God for all the wonderful things He was doing for me.

I was pleased with my stay in Canada. I reconciled with my sister Irène; everything is now fine between us. Jacques and I spent these weeks at my daughter Natatsha's home with our grandchildren. I was glad that Jacques and Patrick, my daughter's husband, got along. The grandchildren got to know their grandfather.

However, the stay was exhausting. I barely had a moment to rest. We had to purchase materials and supplies to be shipped by container. We packed small items into our suitcases. We were completely worn out, especially me. I had a fever and the flu. This time, Jacques returned to Haiti two days before me, giving me a brief chance to rest.

I left Montreal on October 12 and arrived in Haiti very early, at 9:30 a.m. Jacques picked me up at the airport. We went down to Les Cayes the same day. My back hurt.

Leaving my family in Canada was hard this time. I cried, and if I had listened to myself, I would have stayed in Montreal. My heart was heavy, but I knew everyone was well. And I had Jacques waiting for me in Haiti. Moreover, I had to continue with my writing project and the construction plan.

My Journal Entry

We placed the merchandise we had brought from Montreal on the shop shelves. It was a Sunday, a calm day, since our little business was quiet. I thought a lot about my family in Montreal. Time seemed to move slowly.

At the beginning of the week, many customers came because we were unpacking new goods. But afterward, not much was sold. I had the impression that business was not going as well as before. Most people came out of curiosity, without money to buy. Fortunately, we were not relying on this income to live or to continue the construction of the house.

I was beginning to find the town of Les Cayes boring. I was eager to return to Miragoâne. I discussed it with Jacques. He assured me that the following week we would resume the construction project and sell more land, as there were plenty of potential buyers.

Shortly after this conversation, Jacques started making me uncomfortable again. He was clearly nitpicking. He thought I was too calm; even if he did something wrong, I ignored it. I didn't get upset over anything. One day, it escalated into an argument. It was stormy. We didn't speak for two days. I took advantage of this to read. I knew he didn't like it. He expressed his irritation: *"When you read, it's like I don't exist anymore."* Then he observed silence. Meanwhile, I was thinking about my family living in Montreal.

For several days, we did not leave Les Cayes because the truck's transmission was defective. Jacques refused to have anyone repair it except himself.

November 16, 1999   Journal

The holidays are coming soon. I am still in Haiti with Jacques, but I think a lot about my children, my grandchildren, my sister, and my brother Robert, who are back in Montreal. But I cannot be in two places at the same time. I made the choice to stay. My body is in Haiti, yet my mind is in Montreal. I don't know if this is why I've gained weight these past few days. I console myself with food. I know I should stop overeating, but I lack the willpower. I know I need to make an effort; otherwise, my health will suffer.

For the past few days, I've felt a drop in energy. I don't know where it comes from. I haven't returned to writing my memoirs since my return from Montreal. I know I should, but I lack enthusiasm. I don't understand it. I know it will pass. At times, I feel like doing nothing. I hope I'm not slipping back into a depression. *"But no, Enice, forget that!"*

For three days, Jacques has been repairing the transmission of his truck. Roger, the little helper, and I gave him some assistance. He was finally able to finish today after much difficulty, misery, fatigue, and all sorts of complications.

I continue my story

It may be necessary to clarify that Jacques did not want to repair his vehicle himself because of a lack of money. He confided in me that he wanted to inspect its interior and simultaneously test whatever might frighten him. Because he has never been afraid of anything or anyone. And also because he is never afraid of being afraid.

We resumed our quiet little life, with the ups and downs of married life. Until one morning, I received a phone call from my daughter Natatsha, who announced terrible news. For several days, I had been having dreadful nightmares.

I confided to Jacques my premonition that things were not going well in Montreal. He responded that I was being too superstitious.

Sunday, November 30, 1999   Journal

It is 2 a.m. I cannot sleep. My daughter called me at 11:30 p.m. to inform me that my sister Irène's house caught fire and that my brother Robert has been hospitalized with burns covering almost his entire body. He suffered a severe shock. I felt deep sorrow for them. I know my sister well, she often panics for others, and now it has happened to her. She must be in complete distress.

I don't know what to do. Should I leave for Montreal? Immediately, I feel lost. I think about them constantly. I know I should be near them. I am overwhelmed with grief. I must get to Port-au-Prince by 4 a.m. Upon arriving there, I will have much more…

I continue the account regarding the fire

When I informed Jacques about the fire at my sister Irène's house, I observed him out of the corner of my eye. He gave a fleeting smile before sharing his opinion, all while pretending to be surprised. At the moment, I didn't pay much attention to it. I told him of my intention to go see them in Montreal. "After you've spoken with your sister, you'll see whether or not you should go," he suggested.

For the past month, I have had no housemaid. I do everything at home with the assistance of little Roger. Here, it is very difficult to find someone capable of working as a housemaid and who is trustworthy.

Part of my journal

December 15, 1999   journal

Today, December 15, 1999, I think a lot about the accident Jacques had on December 16, 1996. I don't know why. I remember that when the accident happened, I thought he was dead. I believe that God gave him another chance. For me, it was a true miracle. I hoped that he would change his behavior. But no, he has become even more stubborn and cruel toward me. Every time I look at his injured arm, I remember how it happened. Jacques is an obstinate man. He always does things his own way. In my opinion, he should also listen to others from time to time.

I continue my account

After the fire, my sister Irène sent my brother Robert to spend some time in Haiti. He has been in Port-au-Prince at my brother Alain's house for a month. I went to see him and found him unwell. I know when he is not feeling well. I spoke to Alain and recommended that he take Robert to see a doctor. My sister Irène had also sent him money for that purpose.

I have been in Port-au-Prince for five days. Since I am no longer going to Montreal, I am eager to return to Les Cayes to be with my belongings. The week before Christmas, I am usually joyful, since it is a holiday I love. But I already feel that this year will be quiet. I will stay at home with Jacques and little Roger.

I do not know where I will spend New Year's Day, in Montreal or in Haiti. I leave everything in God's hands. Since my return from Montreal, I have not written in my manuscript. I feel a sense of desolation.

Journal December 20, 1999

I am alone in the shop in Les Cayes. Jacques has gone out. These days, I feel very tired because I haven't had a housemaid for a month and a half. I don't have much time for myself. I have to prepare meals, take care of the house and the shop, although little Roger helps me a bit. I find all of this difficult.

Here in Haiti, things don't happen the way they do in Montreal. Everything is much less modern and takes longer to accomplish. It is possible that I will have a housemaid this week before Christmas. She came yesterday for an interview. I found that she seemed like a good person. In any case, I really need her this week before Christmas.

These days, I think about my children and grandchildren, as well as my sister. I suffer greatly from this situation. I think a lot about Montreal because Christmas there is a beautiful celebration. But here in Haiti, it feels as if I'm in a lost hole. The telephone doesn't work. Christmas is too quiet here. I realize that, in the end, it is up to me to do something to make this Christmas joyful. I am thinking about it seriously. I am the one who must create my own happiness.

Part Four

Christmas 1999 in Haiti

Since I now had a housemaid, it became easier for me to plan Christmas Eve and the days that followed. For a time, we paused the construction of the house. I organized sales at discounted prices, lotteries, and many other activities that the local people were not familiar with. We did good business, the clients were satisfied, and I didn't have time to be bored.

Meanwhile, I had scheduled our next trip to Montreal for January 17, 2000. Jacques didn't want to go there for the holidays at all. We had a quiet Christmas in Les Cayes. The housemaid had prepared a nice dinner for the occasion. I couldn't communicate with my children. The millennium was approaching, the year 2000, and according to the media, the country was in total panic. I didn't speak much. I focused my thoughts on my children and grandchildren. In my inner self, in my heart and mind, I was absent.

However, I learned something truly interesting. I was informed that the wife of Jacques's cousin had established a beautiful tradition: every New Year's Day, she serves soup to the poor and anyone in the neighborhood who wants some. She has women prepare the soup in large pots in her garage throughout the night before New Year's Day. The next day, she gives each person a bowl of soup and a small piece of bread.

I remember that on New Year's Eve, I went to Mass. Upon returning, this lady offered me a large bowl of soup to share with my family. That night, we stayed awake to witness the arrival of the new century. Around 2 a.m., we drank the soup before going to bed.

That's how I spent this special New Year's Eve. No champagne, no wine. I was very sad that night. I went out onto the veranda. I looked at the sky, thinking of my family members in Canada. I had a special thought for each of them.

The New Century

New Year's Day 2000

On New Year's Day, we received visitors from Jacques's family, and the mother of little Roger came to ask for money. She told us that one of her sons was ill. In Haiti, when people need money, they can make up any story to get it.

At first, I believed all their stories, even though Jacques warned me. Over the days, I gradually discovered their lies. Despite everything, I continued to help them.

Journal – January 2000

Since the beginning of the new year, I hadn't written anything. Yet, I had so much to share, but my heart wasn't in it. I was deeply saddened. Jacques, however, recognized the sacrifice I had made by staying in Haiti with him during the holidays. He did his best to be kind to me.

For some time, I had been experiencing pain on the left side of my shoulder blade, arm, and chest. During my trip to Montreal, I planned to consult my doctor about this.

I spent Christmas and New Year in Haiti without being able to speak with my children by phone because communication was impossible. This is very common in Haiti.

If I stayed in Haiti, it wasn't because I liked it; it was because of Jacques. He enjoys living in Haiti. I no longer know what to do; I feel deeply troubled.

Construction continues in Chalon. I think things will improve when I have my own house. Actually, I'm not sure anymore. Finally, I was able to communicate with Natatsha. Our trip to Montreal is confirmed for January 17. I am happy at the thought of leaving. We will stay there for three weeks or a little longer.

I continue my story

Two weeks before our departure for Montreal, I hadn't prepared much. I went to visit family and my friend Nelia in Miragoâne, and to check that everything was going well on the land and with the house construction.

Since the end of the holidays, life in Haiti no longer held any meaning for me. It had become a dull routine. I felt a lot of anxiety. I was definitely eager to return to Montreal, especially since my health was worrying me. I felt like a small child, counting the days until my departure.

Part Five

My Stay in Montreal

January 2000

I am happy to be back in Montreal despite the winter. It is very cold here, but I feel very comfortable because there are far fewer germs than in Haiti. I am with my family. I see people, and it is always easier to communicate here.

The day after my arrival, I went to visit my sister Irène. She was happy to see me. While waiting for her house to be repaired, she was staying with her former tenant, Jacobi, who lives in the Outremont neighborhood.

She was well settled there. I told Irène that my brother Robert was not doing well at all in Haiti and that he could not stay there for long. I offered to bring him to Montreal on my next trip to Canada. She agreed with me.

Jacques and I went to see our doctor. He sent us for tests to determine our health status. Fortunately for me, my medical situation was not very serious. The doctor found that I had tendinitis in my left arm. But

Jacques had not yet received his results; he was to get them in a month.

Jacques told me that he would not be able to stay in Montreal for long, partly because of the very cold weather, but also because Érick, a friend from Montreal whose house he was renovating in Haiti, planned to return to the country at the same time to check on the progress of the work. Moreover, Jacques had not finished filling a container destined for Haiti.

One day before his departure for Haiti, my husband had rented a truck to transport goods and materials into the container. Upon his arrival, he found the container locked. It was 10 p.m., and the container owner had already left. Jacques then asked me to stay in Montreal to handle everything the next day. He had to take a flight at 5:30 a.m. At 3 a.m., I drove him to Mirabel Airport. He was very nervous and kept yelling at me, without caring about the people watching us.

When I returned from the airport, since the truck was heavily loaded, I asked my stepson Patrick to drive the large vehicle to the container himself, which he did. I followed him in his car.

Upon our arrival at the dock, the owner was not there yet. It was 8:30 a.m. I got into the truck to wait until noon. I managed to find an employee who helped me load everything into the container. I then drove the truck myself back to the rental office on Pie IX Street, at the corner of Grandes-Prairies. It was 2 p.m. I took the bus to go to my daughter's place on Clarke Street near Crémazie. I arrived there at 4 p.m., very exhausted after such a hard day. The experience really made me reflect. I was actually furious, especially because of how Jacques had treated me at the airport.

During the two weeks I stayed alone in Montreal, I took the opportunity to rest and take care of myself. I felt good. I helped my sister rearrange her house. I was happy to be with my family, keeping out of my mind what awaited me in Haiti. I was overjoyed, in high spirits. But physically, I did not feel very well.

Here is an excerpt from my journal.

March 2007

For a month, I haven't been able to write. I didn't feel like it, even though I had so much to say. Since Jacques left for Haiti, I feel free. Free from this man who takes all my energy.

I remember that when the children were young and we lived as a family, it was as if I had three children to take care of. In truth, he demanded even more from me than the children. When he is not here, I fully enjoy resting my mind and body. Since he didn't want to extend his stay for his medical results, I had to attend the appointment in his place to obtain his prescriptions. The doctor warned me that next time, he must come himself. He gave me the prescriptions because Jacques is diabetic; otherwise, he wouldn't have done it.

For the past few days, I've been thinking about everything I will have to do upon returning to Haiti. My priority will be to finish writing my book as quickly as possible. I have reflected a lot on my way of life in Haiti and on Jacques' behavior. I no longer want to build the house. I fear that after doing it, Jacques will become more aggressive and cause me further misery. I don't need any of that. He is very unpredictable. When he needs something from me, he is very kind. But after a while, he changes.

What I want is to finish my book, return to Montreal to publish it, then have a beautiful, clean apartment, take care of myself, pamper myself a little, and love myself. I would also like to be loved. I no longer want to live in Haiti. It is too hard for me there; I won't get used to it. But for now, what else can I do? I wait.

As for the remaining lands to sell, I would like to do other things with the money I get from them. I pray to God to give me clarity and guide me in my decisions.

When I arrive in Haiti, I will talk to Jacques about all this. I will tell him that I agree to live with him, but that first, I need to finish my book, which is very important to me. And that it is no longer in Haiti that I want to live. I know he won't like that. I won't tell him immediately, but gradually. I think about it a lot.

Part Six

I Arrive Alone in Haiti

The date of my return to Haiti was scheduled for April 5, 2000. I had made this decision without discussing it with anyone. This return was easier than previous times. I felt stronger inwardly.

Jacques was waiting for me at Port-au-Prince airport. I found him in a hurry, and his clothes were dusty. I greeted him. He loaded my luggage into the car and immediately drove toward Les Cayes. I asked him why he was in such a rush. We could have stayed overnight in Port-au-Prince and left for Les Cayes the next day. He refused. He claimed he had things to do in Les Cayes. During the drive, he barely spoke.

When we arrived in Petit-Goâve, the car broke down. The repair took him two hours. I was tired and hungry. Even though I had brought errands for my sister Claire and Nélia, we didn't stop in Miragoâne. Jacques promised it would be next time.

Watching Jacques repair the car, I remarked, "You work hard here in Haiti." He replied: "I'm fine here. I have no problems." I responded: "I find it exhausting, always fixing the cars. Always working, with all this dust and everything else." He retorted: "I like it, that's all." He didn't realize that this lifestyle could harm his health and that a time would come when he could no longer continue.

This time, upon my arrival in Haiti, I found the behavior of those around me rather disconcerting. They were curt and harsh, like the country itself. During the entire trip toward Les Cayes, I looked at the country with sadness. The trees and hills were dry and dull. It hadn't rained for three months. Life had become expensive. It was a disheartening sight.

The day after my return home, I began placing the merchandise I had brought from Canada into the shop. Potential customers hurried to see what was new. Some made small purchases, while others simply looked out of curiosity.

Jacques had other problems with his truck. This forced him to spend his days in the garage repairing it. He was assisted by his nephew Daniel, who had discreetly returned, though I don't know for how long.

As for me, I resumed writing my book with much more seriousness. I was less directly involved with the household chores because I had the help of the maid and little Roger. I would give them instructions on what to do; the rest of the time, I focused entirely on my writing.

Since my return, I hadn't had the time to go to Miragoâne to deliver errands to my sister or to check on the progress of the house construction. I avoided mentioning it to Jacques because I already had my own ideas about it. Finally, we went there on April 15.

"Here is a part of my journal."

Saturday, April 15, 2000

It is 2:30 in the afternoon, and I have been ready since 8 in the morning. I am waiting for Jacques, with whom I am supposed to go to Miragoâne. He told me he needed to fix something on the car before we could leave. Well, that ended up taking the entire day. I took the situation "cool." I made the most of it by writing. Waiting for Jacques had, by now, become a habit for me.

Since I've known him, every time we need to travel, he makes me wait for hours. At first, it was difficult. Sometimes, I would cry. But over the years, and with the support of my cousin Vivianne, who helped me be patient, I eventually got used to it. Thanks also to writing, I was able to pass the time.

I don't even know if we will leave today. If we don't, I will continue working on my memoirs, which I am so eager to finish. Here, I don't have a proper place to write. I have to set up in the shop, where there is always a constant flow of people coming to buy things.

Tuesday, April 18, 2000

I really enjoyed my stay in Miragoâne. This time, my sister Claire was happy to see me again, as was my friend.

My sister remarked to me: *"I went to see the construction; I was glad to see that you are doing something useful with the money from your lands."* But, in fact, I didn't reveal any of my true plans to her.

During my stay in Miragoâne, I was able to sell another piece of land. I still had three others left to sell. But I didn't talk about it. I ultimately decided that I would stop selling for the moment.

Today, I went to pay my electricity bill and deposited the rest of the money in the bank. I am waiting to see what to do next. I now regret having built on the Chalon property. I realized that here in Haiti, nothing is going right anymore. The citizens reflect the state of the country, even if one must be careful not to generalize. I can no longer understand what is happening around me. I am in complete confusion.

I continue the story

We were on April 19, 2000. It was Jacques' birthday. That morning, we stayed in bed a little longer. I had informed the maid that I would let her know when to bring breakfast to our room through little Roger.

I made every effort to ensure that we had a pleasant day. I asked the maid to prepare a nice lunch and had ordered a cake for the occasion, which the maid was supposed to pick up during the day. Right after breakfast, Jacques told me he had to go out because he needed to have an important part welded on the truck. I tried to keep him from leaving, but it was in vain. I still insisted that he come back as soon as possible since I had a pleasant surprise planned for him.

He left at 10:30 a.m. Since it was Holy Week, I had given the maid time off immediately after lunch so she could visit her family. She was supposed to return the next morning because I planned to need her services on Good Friday and Easter Sunday. By the time she left, Jacques had not yet returned. He came back around 4:30 p.m., telling me stories that were clearly fabricated. I didn't say a word. I pretended to listen. I spent the evening writing while he busied himself repairing his truck in the garage. I had dinner alone. I did not mention his outing; it was Holy Week, and I didn't want to be bothered by it.

Since my return from Montreal, the maid had not been feeling well. She kept telling me that she had a stomachache and could not eat. I advised her to see a doctor. I whispered to Jacques that she might be pregnant, but Margot insisted that she was not. I planned to have her examined by a doctor after the Easter holiday. It was mainly because of her persistent stomach pain that I had sent her to visit her family. She left on Wednesday afternoon. She was supposed to return Thursday morning to shop for Good Friday, especially to buy fish. However, she did not return.

I had to do without fish on Good Friday. I felt very frustrated. For once, I would not eat fish on Good Friday. But it wasn't too serious, considering that there are people who have almost nothing to eat. I thought about Margot and assumed her condition might have worsened. She eventually returned around dinner time. She apologized at length. I did not blame her. She promised that the next morning, she would do everything possible to bring me fish or any other seafood. I calmly replied, *"Okay, Margot, that's fine."*

On April 20, 2000, I returned to the house alone with little Roger. As usual, Jacques was out.

Since it was Holy Thursday, I wanted to go to church to attend the foot-washing ceremony. Suze, the wife of Jacques' cousin, told me that the ceremony had already taken place that morning. I no longer understood anything about this country. Everything works backwards, even religious practices. I promised myself that I would go to church on Easter Sunday afternoon.

Sitting in the shop with little Roger, I asked him how things had gone in my absence. He mumbled that everything had gone well. When I asked if the young girl had come to the shop, he told me yes, that she had come to talk to Mr. Jacques and wanted some water. I was satisfied with that information and did not continue the conversation. I remained thoughtful. Once again, I found that Jacques really was not sincere with me.

April 20, 2000 – Journal

I just learned that during my absence, the young girl came to see Jacques in the shop. I find it very inconsiderate of her to show up at my home. Jacques did not mention it to me. He should have said something. I no longer know what to think. It's not jealousy, far from it. It's mainly his hypocrisy that enrages me. But tonight, I will talk to him about it. I'll see what he says.

April 21, 2000 – Journal

I woke up early today. I couldn't sleep. Last night, I spoke to Jacques about the young girl from Cayenne who had come to our house. He replied coldly: *"What does it matter to you?"* He continued: *"Who told you?"* I asked: *"What was she doing here?"* He told me she wanted some water and gave me an invented story. He shouted: *"Why didn't the person who told you explain what really happened?"* And he added: *"I'm at home, I do what I want."* I replied that I did not agree with the young girl coming to our house and that it was his responsibility to inform me of her visit, not someone else's.

I did not continue the conversation further. I felt it was pointless. It became clear that I could no longer trust him fully. He was hiding too much from me, even though I had been sincere with him. I realized I needed to be on my guard; these people could try to harm me at any moment.

Jacques uses the money from my inheritance to pay for everything in the house. He is burning through my capital. I don't know how to react. I have sacrificed so much to come live with him in Haiti. If he is with me, it's only in his own interest. I will never forgive him for what he has done to me because I do not deserve this.

Chapter 11

Betrayal

Part One

A True Breach of Trust

Upon learning this news, I kept my calm. I remained silent. But I thought about it constantly. I noticed that customers were hardly coming to the shop anymore. But I made no connection. I assumed they might be short on money. I decided, nonetheless, to find out more. I went to speak with the maid. I asked her if she had noticed that the young girl came here during my absence. She immediately reacted: "Madame Jacques, I did not come here to watch people." When I insisted, she clarified: "You see, madame, since you returned, you found me sick. Well, madame, my illness is this story that happened in this house. I cannot say more. I asked little Roger to join me in the kitchen. Monsieur Jacques was working in the van at the garage with his cousin Daniel.

I urged the maid and little Roger to tell me everything. They asked me not to reveal their confidences. I gave them my word. They confessed that, since the first day Jacques returned from Montreal, he had sent little Roger to fetch the young girl from her home. She had spent two weeks sleeping at my place. She would come in the evening around 6 o'clock and leave early in the morning. On weekends, she stayed both days. The doors between the kitchen and the shop were locked. Jacques spent all his time with her. The maid sent Roger to bring the three meals upstairs. He would place the tray in front of the bedroom door. No one was allowed to enter. Whenever Jacques went to Port-au-Prince, upon his return, even if it was late, he had the young girl fetched. The two lovers watched television and laughed almost constantly.

Informed of all these facts, I felt that Jacques had no shame: putting a woman in my bed, in my personal matters, in my private life. I was ashamed for myself and for him as well. Without my husband knowing, I asked Roger and the maid to accompany me to my room. I took a pair of scissors and a sharp knife. I tore the mattress, then the pillow. With their help, I then ordered them to throw everything into the street. In the blink of an eye, the poor people of the neighborhood had collected everything.

Having observed the scene, Jacques came to join me in the office demanding an explanation. I revealed to him that I was aware of everything that had happened during my absence. He stared at me without uttering a word. In fact, he was trying to hide his embarrassment. He abruptly returned to work in the garage.

But at that moment, I no longer knew how to behave. I resisted the urge to call my daughter. Not immediately, at least.

At the same time, the temptation to flee came to mind. I rushed to my room. I was about to pack my bags. All in all, I was struggling with another part of myself. The intense desire to run away was growing. I was very nervous; my whole body was trembling. I kept repeating to myself: "I have to do something." I went down to the shop. I took the key, opened the desk drawer, and part of me determined to take my passport and run away. I reasoned with myself: "Enice, don't run away, stay, you have to stay to help me finish my book. I want to reach my goal."

My right hand brushed against the passport. I couldn't even touch it. It was a battle between me and my other self. An extremely painful moment. I did not cry. My brain worked like a clock to the second, but in disorder. I was alone with my other self, who only wanted to leave.

Finally, I shouted forcefully: No! And I closed the desk drawer. I went to Suze, Jacques's cousin's wife.

We settled on the balcony. I confided in her about what Jacques had done to me. Of course, she already knew. She acknowledged that she had been aware of everything since the first week Jacques returned from Montreal: "Everyone in town is talking about it, and if your maid is sick, it's because of that." She thought it necessary to add: "If you notice that people no longer come to buy at the shop, it's because they are afraid of upsetting you and they no longer have the same respect for Jacques as before." She wanted to know what I planned to do. I told her I would think about it. She wished me good luck, and I returned home. My visit had lasted half a day.

When I got back home, I closed the shop. I went up to my room. I felt explosive. I took a calming medicine and prayed to God. Then I decided to make myself a bed. Since there was a double mattress left in the room, I placed it on a large bed frame and fashioned pillows out of blankets and sheets. It wasn't comfortable, but at least I could sleep for the time I still intended to spend in this house.

In the evening, I called Jacques. I told him that I wanted to speak with him. He lingered before coming upstairs.

When I tried to speak to him about his absurdities with the teenage girl, he refused to discuss it: "Forget all that," he told me, "I don't want to hear about it anymore." I was sad; I felt I was about to burst at any moment. I couldn't take it anymore. Especially his contemptuous attitude.

Here is what I wrote about that night

April 24, 2000

Today is Easter Monday. Last night, I did not sleep well. I spent part of the night pacing back and forth in the room because I had had enough. I felt like screaming and killing, like breaking everything within my reach. I was in great pain. I could not imagine Jacques bringing this girl or any other girl into my room, into our bed, into my private life. Oh no! I did not want to believe it. It was stronger than me. I felt like I was about to faint. I screamed with all my strength.

I had a crisis. It felt as though my heart wanted to burst out of my chest. Jacques woke up. He gave me a tranquilizer while asking what was wrong. He already knew very well what was wrong. I still asked him why he had done such a filthy thing. What harm had I ever done to him? Usually, it is when things are not going well that he behaves badly to get my attention.

This time, he put my life in danger. I cannot accept that. From now on, I must rely only on myself.

I still do not know what to do, but I am thinking about it seriously. Instead of torturing me, Jacques should adore me. I put everything in God's hands. Yet, at the same time, many bad ideas are crowding my mind. For example, killing him and then fleeing to Montreal but I prayed about it, and the good Lord heard me. I know He will guide me so that I make the right decision. In the meantime, I continue writing my book.

I had tried at all costs to forget this story in order to focus on writing my book. I intended not to speak about it to the children because it was too shameful. I had even removed my other troubling thoughts from my mind so I could devote myself entirely to writing. But the very next day, I learned news of another incident just as serious.

Here is part of my journal:

Journal – April 25, 2000

Today is yet another dreadful day for me. I have learned that every day Jacques would take the young girl out of town to have a good time. He would take her to the beach, while he never takes me out. They arranged to meet behind her house, while I was tending the shop, poor innocent me.

Clearly, I can no longer endure anything from this man. I know I no longer love him. The young girl apparently said that she was waiting for me to leave or die so she could marry Jacques. I know that all of Jacques's outings were hiding lies. For example, when he went to have his truck or car welded, I sensed that he was lying to me. To avoid problems, I did not react. But what hurts me the most is that I cannot speak to my children about it. I am too ashamed of myself. This time, I am not thinking about suicide. I am thinking of revenge. I do not know how, but I am not worrying about it. I will find a way and the right moment to act.

Now, I no longer trust Jacques. I am certain that whenever he opens his mouth, it is to tell lies. On his birthday, he went to meet the young girl, pretending he had an important work appointment. He returned five hours later. Such a man does not deserve to be appreciated. This new information has made me think a great deal.

I continue my story.

After getting this information, I felt the hatred grow in my heart. I tried to talk to Jacques to find out the truth. He claimed that for him, it was in the past and he no longer wanted to discuss it. I insisted on the importance of such a clarification. "Why do you care about a little girl who means nothing at all?" he retorted. He and I had other much more serious matters to attend to.

He tried to make me believe that he had never slept with the young girl. During the exchange, he expressed his desire for us to make love. I refused. He insisted physically. Once he got what he was aiming for, I felt that I no longer had any feelings for him. I was like a frigid woman. He tried to be nice to me because he was afraid I would give up on building the house. For my part, I had not given up on my revenge. I kept thinking about it.

For some time, I had been struggling to sleep through the night. I felt morally tired. I managed to function as usual, but with less enthusiasm. When the vendors and customers came to the store, I hardly spoke to them, the enthusiasm was no longer there. It was then that I realized that I no longer wanted to stay in Haiti. I no longer had a place in this country. One day, I went out on the gallery; the young girl came out on hers, and she immediately spewed nonsense at me. I pretended not to hear her. I went back inside. I felt humiliated. I told Jacques about the incident. He showed no reaction.

From then on, I could no longer understand how I could have loved a man like him. I also realized more and more that he was nothing of a real man, that he was on the contrary a worthless little man. He had become dangerously aggressive again. He pretended to be always fixing his van. On several occasions, I had suggested that he take the van to a mechanic. But according to him, no one really knew mechanics in Haiti. He was always right.

April 29, 2000

It is noon. Last night, we went to bed very late because we had to finish the computerized production of advertising brochures to be delivered today. We work late into the night because during the day, Jacques is busy with the van. He is rebuilding the radiator. For the past three weeks, he has been working on it with his nephew Daniel. He does not want to listen to anyone. It is always his way that is right; he cannot be advised. Watching him closely, I judge that he is, after all, exhausting himself.

Last night, he seemed very nervous to me. He could not concentrate. I pretended not to notice. But when he woke up this morning, he admitted that he had not slept well. I reassured him: "I think that's normal. You have too many things to do at once the van mechanics, the container arriving in Port-au-Prince, the work at the La Boule house, the construction of the house in Chalon, etc." I wonder how he manages to have so much fun with the young girl so often.

Regarding the construction in Miragoâne, I do not think this house will ever be finished. For me, it is a thing of the past; I forget this project. I have not yet mentioned it to Jacques. My silence is part of my plan. Although I had the intuition that he was lying to me when he left after dinner to return after supper, I did not risk making any comment. But I learned that he was bringing the young girl to my house, into my bed, and I noticed semen stains on the sofa cushions in the living room. That is when I reacted. Not out of jealousy, far from it. Because I feared for my life, I realized that I was in real danger. I had to do something. But first, let us think about revenge.

Part Two

Desire for Revenge and Spiritual Interventions

Since the incident of April 20, 2000, I have not changed my way of life. I continued to take care of my affairs as if nothing had happened. I spoke and laughed with people as usual, all the while hiding my inner feelings. To the point that my maid reported the following remarks from some people: "How is it that madame did not make a scene with her husband and the young girl?"

These same people continued: "Is that how things work in her country, Canada?" I then instructed the maid not to involve herself in this matter any longer. For almost a month, I had been suffering terribly and in silence. I had revealed nothing to my children nor to my friend in Miragoâne. In any case, I had no desire to go to Miragoâne at all.

I nurtured and worked on my plan for revenge in my mind. My heart ached. The wound was raw. One day, I realized I could no longer bear it. I had to speak to my daughter, particularly about my plan. I waited until I was alone in the shop to call Natatsha. I revealed to her the essential details of what had happened. She was stunned to hear the news. "Since then, you should have called me," she gently reproached me. "You must come back to Montreal. You will be fine; don't stay in Haiti."

I immediately responded: "No, I am not returning to Montreal right away. Before I go, I will kill Jacques; immediately after, I will take the plane to Montreal." She asked at once: "Are you sure you can do it?" I confirmed to her: "Yes, I already have my plan. That is why I had not called you sooner. Besides, I was ashamed of myself." She advised me to be very vigilant and to confide in no one. I assured her: "I have revealed nothing to anyone, not even to your brother Max." And I concluded: "Don't worry about anything; I have the money for my plane ticket. Pray for me.

In the meantime, I continued living with Jacques.

We went on a trip to Miragoâne. I confided the painful situation to my sister Claire, but I also spoke about it to her husband, my brother-in-law, and to my friend Nélia. They, in turn, strongly condemned Jacques's behavior.

Jacques and I had planned a stay in Port-au-Prince for at least three weeks. Our plan was to clear the container and finish the work on the La Boule house with the whole team: the maid, little Roger, and my husband's nephew. The trip was scheduled for May 18.

My plan was to kill Jacques four days before our departure for Port-au-Prince. I had planned everything. Everything was ready for the execution. I was very kind to him. He suspected nothing. I felt no trace of remorse. This man had caused me too much suffering over all these years. I was completely at my limit. I had spent the majority of my life with him, hoping that one day he would change. The change never came. And every time I left him, he came back for me. I could no longer bear it; my decision was made. I would kill him. I had nourished this idea so much that I could no longer remove it from my mind.

My plan was to be carried out in the morning. The day before the event, it was 7 p.m.; I was upstairs, sitting in the living room. I was watching television, but my mind was elsewhere. I was thinking about what I would have to do the next morning. Suddenly, I noticed that a biblical movie was being broadcast on TV, *The Ten Commandments*. I was alone; Jacques was in the bedroom. I immediately thought: "Why are they showing *The Ten Commandments* today? They must be crazy." But since I love the story of the film, I decided to watch it without ulterior motives.

Moses began reading the Ten Commandments. When he pronounced this one: "You shall not kill your neighbor," I heard his voice so strong, deep, and distant. It was as if he were speaking directly to me. I shivered and got up from the sofa. I went downstairs and sat at the desk. I took my Bible and prayed. I read a few passages from the Bible.

I felt a gentle inner peace. The hatred had disappeared.

I was calm and happy. I went upstairs. Jacques was already asleep. I lay down and slept until morning. I felt full of energy. I asked the maid to go shopping for supplies for the trip to Port-au-Prince. I prepared the luggage.

I had decided to go to Port-au-Prince in order to work on my book. To do this, I had to make the sacrifice of living with Jacques as if I were in my twenties. To write this new part of my book, I had to banish hatred from my heart. Otherwise, I was mentally frozen. I thanked God for preventing me from committing this grave mistake. I thanked Him for listening to me, since at the beginning of this story, I had begged Him to guide me on what to do. He had heard me and revealed the right path. He saved my soul and Jacques's life, because if I had killed him, I would have been forced to carry that burden for my entire life. And my daughter, in turn, would have been forced to keep that heavy secret to protect me. I do not think I would have had the courage to do it. I was confused; my other self had almost completely taken over. The circumstances of this matter remain a mystery. And that evening, it was a miracle. I will never forget that voice.

This whole experience led me to step into the skin of a twenty-year-old woman in order to write my memoirs and complete my first book.

Part Three

Our Stay at La Boule

(End of writing Volume I)

We left for Port-au-Prince on May 18.

Throughout the journey, I was anxious. I wanted to reach our destination as quickly as possible because I was eager to begin writing and to breathe the fresh air of La Boule, on the mountainside. Despite the minor problems we encountered along the way, the trip went smoothly. I was eager to put my plans into action. Before recounting my stay at La Boule, I would like to give my readers an idea of what I intended to do and why. I had planned to return to the past of my twenties, to immerse myself in the skin of a young, fresh, and beautiful girl, overflowing with sensuality.

To successfully narrate this past I had shared with my first husband and especially with Jacques; to continue writing the first segment of my life, as I reached the sixth chapter of *A Woman Among Many Others*; to meet this great challenge, I had to erase all traces of hatred from my heart. I intended to bring out all my feelings. I admit it was a tough trial for me. But I completed the process to prevent readers from sensing my insecurity. I followed it with all my heart.

While writing this part of my life, I made sure to take care of myself both spiritually and physically. I was calm, in love, smiling, happy and it showed. But one thing was off: I suffered a loss of energy at the end of each writing session; however, I did not worry about it. Despite that, I was able to continue cheerfully. The more I made love, the more ideas flowed. In this way, I regenerated myself. I wanted to reach my goal at all costs. That is why I was so eager to come to La Boule, a haven of tranquility and far from the negative world.

Here is what I wrote the day after my arrival at La Boule.

May 19, 2000 – Journal

Today is Friday, and I am at La Boule in the large house that Jacques is to renovate. I am here with Jacques, little Roger, Claudy, and his brother, as well as my maid Margot.

We had a good trip. Upon arriving in Port-au-Prince, we visited my uncle George. I brought provisions for his wife, which she greatly appreciated. We then went up to La Boule before sunset. I was delighted to enter the house of my dreams. I can hardly believe it, I will be spending three weeks here; it is true happiness for me. At least during these three weeks, I will be able to finish my manuscript.

After giving some instructions to the maid, the first thing I did was go up to the bedroom with Margarethe and Roger. They swept it to remove the dust, and we prepared the bed because I knew well that as soon as Jacques came up, he would go to bed. And that is indeed what he did. We rested a little. I asked the maid to prepare dinner in the meantime. When we went downstairs, Jacques set the table, the radio, etc. With the help of Roger and Margot, we put away the provisions, the dishes, the pots, and tidied up the kitchen.

After dinner, around 8:30 p.m., we took our baths and went to bed. We were in a good mood and chatted until 10 p.m. Jacques still said he was tired and felt pain all over, especially in his feet, knees, and back. I advised him to do some stretching, which helped him feel better. Around 10:30, we began caressing each other and made love. I found him more relaxed. Even I let myself go, something I hadn't dared to do for a long time.

Here at La Boule, we enjoy a greater calm than in Les Cayes. When I was in our house in Les Cayes, I didn't feel comfortable. It was as if that house were haunted. Here, I feel well; even my thoughts are clearer. I think I should no longer live there. Last night, while making love with Jacques, he confided that he thought I pleased him better.

What he hadn't noticed was that I was not the same woman. I was becoming again that sensual and gentle woman of the past.

In any case, during these three weeks, I will do everything possible to reach my goal. This morning, I didn't feel like getting out of bed. I felt good, especially in this large room surrounded by windows, unlike in Les Cayes, where the room has no windows. Without a fan, we could never sleep there.

Jacques woke up before me; usually, I am the one who wakes up earlier. This time, he suggested that I stay in bed.

I got up anyway to be able to contemplate nature, pray, and write. I feel good here. I will be able to finish my book. Jacques said he had slept well. He teased me a little about our performance last night. When I went downstairs, the guys had already had their coffee. They greeted me and told me they had slept well and that they liked the place. I had breakfast with Jacques. Then I went upstairs to get dressed and organize my things. Afterward, I took my bag containing my writing accessories and my prayer book. I informed Jacques: "If you need me, I'm in the yard."

Once on the terrace, I settled under a mango tree to get some shade and to have a view over the green mountains. The first thing I did was pray to God, asking Him to grant me the inspiration to write and to protect my children and grandchildren. I took a deep breath and meditated for a few minutes. I am now beginning to write the beginning of chapter six of my book. Until tomorrow.

Part Four

The Writing Work, Book 1

This is how I continued with my writing plan.

For several days, it was the same routine. I was always outside writing. Between my writing sessions, I would walk around the yard to stretch my legs. The weather was always beautiful, nature was lovely, and I felt inspired.

I thought only of executing my project. At night, it was different. I nourished myself with something else. The maid, on the other hand, took care of everything. She knew what to do. For me I was alone in a large house. I saw the other occupants as blurred figures. I was in another world, a world of the past.

I remember one day the maid tried to ask me something. I was writing outside. She stood next to me. She spoke to me and called my name, but I didn't hear her. When she touched me, it was as if I had fallen into emptiness. I jumped, and she got scared. She immediately explained: "Excuse me, madam, but I've been here a long time. I called you, but you didn't hear, that's why I touched you." I told her not to worry. Everything was fine.

Meanwhile, Jacques was working with his nephews. Everything went smoothly. When he went to town, I accompanied him because I was afraid of being alone in the house. I also took the opportunity to call my children, since the house did not have a telephone. It happened to be election time in Haiti, so people were wary of home invasions.

Journal – May 21, 2000

Today is Sunday, election day in Haiti. I am at La Boule. This morning, I woke up a little late. We went downstairs for breakfast. Then I went upstairs to wash my undergarments and organize the room so I could write safely inside, while any disorder could erupt in the streets during election time.

Around noon, I went to the kitchen to check how Margot was managing with lunch. Everything was fine. She knew her work well. After lunch, around 2 p.m., I went out into the yard. I settled not too far from the house, as a precaution. In a spot clearly visible to Jacques and the guys more precisely, right near an avocado tree.

Yesterday, we went into town to make some purchases and make phone calls. I noticed that food costs more in Port-au-Prince than in the provinces. In general, life is very expensive in Haiti. We went to Rémonde's, Jacques's sister, to make phone calls. Jacques intended to call his business partner to check if the container had arrived. It had, indeed, arrived. I took the opportunity to call my daughter, but she was not home. I managed to speak with Patrick, her husband. He told me that Natatsha had tried to call me several times, but no phone line was working in Haiti. I needed to call her back because she needed me. Patrick's urging made me very worried.

Nevertheless, we went to have lunch at a restaurant in Delmas. We ordered hamburgers and lemonade. We gave a little money to the maid and to Roger so they could buy food of their choice.

When we returned home, Jacques took a short nap. I helped Margot prepare something for dinner. We dined outside in the yard and stayed there until bedtime.

I continue my story

As I have already noted, each day I took a short 30-minute walk in the yard. At the same time, I admired the nature, the wooded mountains, and the imposing houses scattered around. All of this made me dream. I freed my mind while looking at the sky. One would have thought it was close to me. It was as if I were in paradise. I then decided to make the most of the time I would spend in this house, which I had wished to be mine.

During my stay at La Boule, I did not speak again about the very painful incident in Les Cayes. But that was not because I had forgotten it far from it! Simply, I was determined to focus on writing my book, which I intended to finish before my departure for Montreal. That departure had been scheduled for June 30, 2000. I therefore had one month left to achieve my goal.

In life, however, one cannot plan everything to the letter. A fortuitous event came to change my plan.

Here is what happened (I noted it in my journal).

May 24, 2000   Journal

We woke up early to call Natatsha. I was able to reach her; she had an important message to communicate to me. I was to return to Montreal the following week, the week of June 2. It was as if I had anticipated her message.

While leaving Les Cayes, I had brought my passport in case I needed it or had to return urgently to Montreal. On our way to Port-au-Prince, Jacques realized that he had forgotten the suitcase containing the passport on the table. I admit that I had been careless. I should have taken care of everything myself. Next time, I will know how to handle it.

I continue my story

I had to return to Les Cayes to retrieve my passport and organize my personal belongings before leaving for Montreal. I was going to Montreal alone for only a week. Jacques would remain in Haiti to handle the customs clearance of the container and continue the construction work. I didn't mind this arrangement. He could do as he pleased with his young mistress; I didn't care. My only concern was this trip to Montreal, after which I would return to finish my book. It so happened that I had other projects in mind.

We spent two days in Les Cayes, and by May 30, we were already in Port-au-Prince. The trip was scheduled for June 2, 2000. I took advantage of the two days of waiting at La Boule to write down some reflections in my journal.

Here is what I wrote.

June 2, 2000 – Journal

It is 2:40 a.m.; the flight is scheduled for 5:30 a.m. I am at the airport in Haiti, all alone. Jacques came to drop me off and has already left. I feel fine. I am not worried about him; I know he will manage during my absence.

Since the sad incident, I no longer trust him, so I don't care what he does or doesn't do. In any case, despite this trip to Montreal, my focus is above all on my book. I did, however, remind him to watch his actions during my stay in Montreal.

On the other hand, I am happy to leave because I am eager to see my family. I will be able to rest. I leave in peace because Margot, the maid, is a responsible person; she knows what to do.

I don't understand Jacques at all. He does not take his responsibilities seriously. I am the one who takes care of everything. It is with the money from the sale of land that he covered the customs clearance of the container, the registration of the truck, etc. Therefore, I had to make withdrawals from my own account before leaving to pay for everything, including the lease of the house in Les Cayes. Clearly, I need to better supervise my affairs; otherwise, I won't have a penny left.

Part Five

A Short Stay Alone in Montreal

I returned to Montreal on June 2nd to go back to Haiti on June 9th, 2000. I therefore stayed in Montreal for one week. I described my schedule during this week in my journal. Here it is.

June 6, 2000   Journal

I arrived in Montreal on June 2 at 10:50 PM. I was very happy to see Natatsha, Patrick, and the two children. They, in turn, were very glad to have me there. Natatsha hugged me tightly. Patrick was upstairs with the children.

She went to get them. When they came down, Elle-Camay jumped into my arms. Mikaël, on the other hand, didn't hug me immediately; he just asked to see his grandfather: "Where is grandpa?" He looked around, hoping to see his grandfather at any moment. When he realized he wasn't with me, he finally decided to hug me.

We had a light meal. Then Natatsha and I talked all night. We went to bed at 4:30 AM. I didn't sleep long. I felt tired and very weak. I got up at 6:30 AM. I had slept in Elle-Camay's room. The children were delighted to have me with them. I helped Natatsha sew her daughter's costume for her ballet performance. She also needed to make a dress for attending a friend's wedding.

When it was time to go to the wedding, I left at the same time as her. We had agreed that she would drop me off at my sister Irène's house and come back to pick me up after the wedding.

When I arrived at my sister's, she had visitors, two friends I knew, and my brother Robert, who lives with her, was also present. It was dinner time. We all sat down to eat. During dinner, our conversation focused mainly on Haiti.

Once her guests had left, Irène noticed that I looked tired and suggested I rest a bit. She invited me to lie down in her large bed; since I was cold, she helped me put on socks and gave me a sweater to keep warm. We chatted for a long time. She then came to lie down next to me, and we fell asleep immediately. We woke up at the sound of the telephone; it was midnight. It was Natatsha calling to let me know she would come to pick me up. I would have preferred to stay at my sister's, but that wasn't possible since the next day was Elle-Camay's ballet performance.

The next morning, June 4, I woke up around 10 AM. I spent a calm, pleasant morning. We got ready to leave at 2:30 PM for Elle-Camay's performance, which was scheduled for 3:30 PM.

It was a beautiful classical and tap ballet performance. Elle-Camay performed very well. After the show, we went to the hospital to visit Patrick's aunt, who was ill. When I entered her room, I was shocked to see her. She was unrecognizable, even though it had only been two months since I had last seen her. I didn't want to go into the room.

I counted on the fact that the lady was not one of my acquaintances and that she did not know I would come to visit her. All things considered, I did not regret going. Seeing this woman fall into such a state so quickly made me reflect deeply. I adopted the following motto for myself: "I must think of myself first, and others afterward."

After careful reflection, I made this weighty decision. So, my decision is made: "I will no longer live as a couple in Haiti with Jacques. Upon my return to that country, I will spend two weeks preparing my bags to return permanently to Montreal."

As for Jacques, he will do as he pleases. I know his temperament, so I will not reveal a single word of my decision to him as long as I am in Haiti. This resolution gave me a renewed energy. I chose to act this way to preserve my health first. It's not that I don't love Haiti, but

Jacques makes me endure too much there. I carry very bitter memories of all this.

Upon leaving the hospital, we went to have dinner at a restaurant. It was about time because I was very hungry and felt very weak. We ate well. As soon as I arrived home, I went to bed, anticipating a busy day the next Monday.

On Monday, June 5, I went to see my doctor. My health was worrying me. He sent me to have some tests done. I didn't know if I would get the results before my departure. I spent the whole day outside. Since I didn't have a car, I used public transportation. I did some shopping. When I returned home, I went out again, this time with Natatsha, with whom I went to pick up the children from daycare. We spent a quiet evening with them.

Last night, I had a dreadful nightmare. I woke up screaming, "Bless the Lord!" In this frightening dream, I saw a woman who wanted to harm me. From that point, I remained awake from 1:00 a.m. I could no longer sleep. Around 2:30 a.m., I prayed and kept my rosary with me.

June 9, 2000   Journal

Today is Friday. I am returning to Haiti after spending a week in Montreal, an extremely exhausting week due to all the appointments. I felt drained, especially since I had to help my daughter with her children.

For the past three days, I haven't had time to write. On Wednesday evening, I went to stay at my sister's. I had a good time with her. Today, it was Natatsha who came to take me to the airport. I felt both sad and happy at the same time because I knew I wouldn't be staying long in Haiti.

I reflected on my situation: I can no longer travel as I used to; it tires me too much. I need to make arrangements to lead an orderly life.

First of all, I aim to finish my book. Then, I will put my decision into action. My health no longer allows me to live under the same conditions in Haiti with Jacques. I can no longer fight with him. He is a man who thinks only of himself. In fact, he repeats it constantly. He always does what he wants. As for me, my decision will remain irreversible.

Despite everything, I had a good stay in Montreal. My only regret is that I didn't see Max and his family. But we spoke very often on the phone, and everything is going well for them.

I don't know what surprise awaits me in Haiti. Has Jacques resumed his sexual encounters with his young mistress in our house?

Part Six

A Final Stay in Haiti with Jacques

Upon my return to Haiti, Jacques was waiting for me. Since I planned to spend very little time in the country only twenty days I had to accelerate the writing of my book. We stayed seven more days at La Boule, just enough time for Jacques to finish his construction work. Meanwhile, I took advantage of the time to write. Due to all my previous travels, I felt exhausted, which prevented me from giving 100% to my writing activity.

My daughter had bought me natural health products that helped me a lot. I wrote almost all day, about ten hours daily, taking only breaks for lunch or dinner. In the evenings at bedtime, Jacques and I would discuss what we needed to do the next day or in the future. These discussions always ended with sex sessions. However, I no longer desired him; the awakening I had felt before going to Montreal had disappeared. I was obliged to pretend. Especially upon my return from Montreal, during our conversations, I noticed that he was still the same man.

Above all, he claimed to always be right. He made a point of making me bear the burden of everything that had gone wrong in our married life. I let him talk because, in any case, my plan to break away had been firmly decided since Montreal. Concerned with protecting myself, I intended to reveal it to him only once I was back in Montreal. Otherwise, he would have made my life miserable in Haiti.

Very cautiously, I suggested suspending the construction of the house and resuming it after our return to Montreal. I also pointed out that we had surplus merchandise. Upon arriving in Les Cayes, we could sell off this excess. He thought the idea was good.

We therefore returned to Les Cayes a week later to implement the plan. At the same time, I discreetly sorted the luggage I would bring to Montreal, so as not to arouse Jacques's suspicion. By the time we left La Boule, I had almost finished my book; I was writing the final chapter. If necessary, I would complete it in Montreal. At this decisive stage of my life, I tried to avoid any unnecessary stress.

For the five-day clearance sale, we spread a large part of the stock out on the veranda, meanwhile closing the shop to prepare for our departure. We informed our clients that we would be leaving for four months. In response to their persistent questions about my plans to return, I repeatedly told them: "Yes, I'm coming back; if I'm leaving, it's because of a health issue." My daughter called me on June 24 to let me know that my doctor had called. He had just received the test results and wanted to see me as soon as possible. I informed her that I would return on June 30 and asked her to schedule an appointment accordingly.

On June 27, 2000, we packed our bags. I was jubilant leaving Les Cayes. I didn't want to hold on to any bad memories. For me, this part of my life was already in the past. I felt no regret. As I left, I didn't look back. Throughout the journey, I remained calm and composed. I passed through Miragoâne to say goodbye to my friend Nélia, as well as to my sister and brother-in-law. My sister Claire was delighted to see that I was returning to Montréal. In conclusion, I was happy to put an end to these continuous comings and goings. I felt the relief of shedding an immense burden.

June 28, 2000 – Journal

Today, I am in Port-au-Prince. I haven't written for a few days, especially not in my book. I haven't had the time because there were too many things to take care of. I returned yesterday, and I'm leaving for Montréal in two days. I plan to use this interval to write a little. But I am so tired that I wonder if I will even be able to write. If not, I will finish whatever remains in Montréal.

Yesterday, the morning I left for Port-au-Prince, Jacques' young mistress called me to apologize for having thrown nonsense at me on the gallery. I told her that I hadn't heard her. I thought she was talking to herself.

She claimed that she was not responsible for any of this and that it was Jacques who had forced her to come sleep at my place. I told her I didn't want to know anything about the story. She cried on the phone, complaining about being a poor girl to whom Jacques had caused a lot of harm, and so on. I advised her to discuss it with him. I was about to hang up when she whimpered, "I'll send you my address; please, when you're in Canada, send me a little money." As her sobs grew louder, I cut it short and hung up. I felt a little pity for her. Fifteen minutes later, a little girl came to give me the address.

I worked a lot during these three weeks I spent in Haiti. I feel exhausted; I need rest. When I arrive in Montréal, the first thing I will do is rest. I am eager to be with my family because in Haiti, I don't live, I survive. There, life is full of abuse and problems.

I returned to Haiti believing that Jacques was serious when he told me he loved me and couldn't live without me. But I realized he was using me to achieve his own ends. He lied to me. He only cared about his interests and petty pleasures. From now on, in Montréal, I will think of myself first. I know he expects me to return to live with him in Haiti, but for me, it's over. If he really wants me, he will come live with me in Montréal. And then, I will not let him treat me the way he did before. At first, it will be difficult, but gradually I will reclaim my place.

I acknowledge that in Les Cayes, the people in the neighborhood were kind to me; I had no problems with anyone. Roger, my little protégé, went to his parents while waiting for my return. I didn't dare tell him that I would not be coming back.

I cared for that little boy; he is endearing. I will never forget him. I know that the Lord will watch over him. He was happy to visit his family. He needed it. I gave him gifts and money for him and his mother. The maid accompanied us to Port-au-Prince. After our departure, she can do as she wishes, but I think Jacques wants to keep her. All of that no longer concerns me. Jacques is very strict with her, but that's how things are in Haiti. There are even people who mistreat domestic workers. That's not my way.

I think this will be the last time I write in my journal while in Haiti. Next time, it will be in Montréal. I will use the two remaining days here to admire the nature, buy souvenirs for my family in Montréal, and say goodbye to my loved ones in Port-au-Prince.

Farewell, dear Haiti. I love you, but at this moment, I can no longer stay with you. I have gained many experiences and used this time to learn about your culture and people. One day, I will return. You should never say never. I leave you now, Haiti. (June 30, 2000)

Chapter 12

Definitive Return to Montréal

Part One

Returning to Montréal on June 30, 2000

Before returning to Montréal, I had converted the little Haitian money I had left from my inheritance into U.S. dollars. Upon arrival, I decided to organize my life to be fully autonomous. I felt it was important to own a car. I discussed it with my daughter, and she agreed that it was the right decision. I resolved to purchase a vehicle with my inheritance money, at least to keep a tangible memory of it. However, the amount I had was not enough to pay for the car in full.

My son-in-law and daughter accompanied me to various dealerships to choose a vehicle. I opted for a beige Nissan van. I made a down payment, and the remaining balance was set over 24 months. I had also set aside money for insurance and registration. Everything was ready. I hadn't mentioned a word to Jacques about it. He was supposed to return Friday evening, and I had planned to surprise him by picking him up at the airport in my new vehicle. In the meantime, I rested a little, knowing I needed strength before resuming my writing project.

My daughter had meanwhile informed me that she had found someone who could guide me through the process of writing and producing the book. I asked her to allow me three weeks to finish and revise the manuscript before meeting my potential collaborator.

On Friday, July 7, I went to pick up Jacques at the airport. As soon as he saw the vehicle, he asked, "Who does it belong to?" I told him it was mine, that I had just bought it. He wanted to know with what money. I explained everything in detail. His reaction was: "Tomorrow, I'll go with you to the dealership to change the car." He added that I should have chosen a second-hand car, cheaper and smaller. I replied that it was precisely a small four-cylinder vehicle and that I wanted no other. He did not appreciate my stance.

Back at home, I went to speak with my daughter about the situation. She approved my reply: "Mammy, don't let him push you around. You've hardly received anything from your inheritance. I think you did well to buy this van. You must stand your ground."

Jacques and I were staying in the basement of my daughter's house. We had rented it from my son-in-law. In fact, we could use the entire house. The basement still did not have a bathroom.

When I went back downstairs, Jacques immediately pressed me again. He harassed me so much that I finally conceded: "Okay, tomorrow we'll go to the dealership."

We went. I presented the problem to my salesperson. He agreed that I could take another vehicle. But Jacques chose a small, battered car. I grumbled, "You can buy it for yourself because I don't see myself in it." And I continued, "You know, my friend, I'm keeping my little van. I'll manage to pay for it each month. You do what you want." I then apologized to the salesperson while notifying him that I was keeping my vehicle.

At first, my husband was upset, but I managed to convince him that, in the end, it was better to buy a car in good condition to avoid continual repair costs. I promised him he wouldn't have to worry at all about the van's monthly payments.

From the second week after my return to Montreal, I set to work to finish my manuscript and revise it.

Throughout the month of July, I was therefore unable to write in my journal. I also did not have much time to monitor Jacques's actions. Finally, during the first week of August, Natatsha and I met with the editor Julie Martino at the Charters bookstore in downtown Montreal, at 6 p.m.

Once introductions were made, I explained everything to her, emphasizing how precious the manuscript was to me. I handed her the two notebooks that revealed my most intimate secrets. I was hesitant, and she noticed. For the moment, I was only offering her the typed transcription of the manuscript. She agreed to sign a confidentiality agreement. We agreed on a price for the transcription and a deadline.

She was supposed to provide me with seven copies of the transcribed manuscript by a set date, in order to gauge interest through a readers' panel. She swore to me that she was trustworthy and that my manuscript was in good hands.

Upon leaving, I felt relieved: "I feel that I will be able to trust her and work with her," I thought. The chemistry had clearly clicked between us.

Max and Natatsha started brainstorming a title for the book, a preliminary step before initiating copyright procedures. We also had to look for a publisher, but not before the readers' panel gave us their evaluation. Money, as is often said, is the lifeblood of any venture. However, I was almost out of money, having spent nearly everything on Jacques in Haiti. In short, I was virtually broke. Still, I managed to pay my rent, my car, groceries, and my phone.

Meanwhile, Jacques was being very nice to everyone. He played with the grandchildren, spent long hours at his computer, and did nothing else. He offered me no help with the upkeep of the apartment. I had to take care of everything. And at night, he still demanded sexual relations.

He finally noticed that I had changed. He now had to insist to get his share of sex. One day, he brought up the subject: "During the last month we spent in Haiti, you were very sensual and warm when we made love. How come you've become so cold now?" I replied, "It's like this, I don't know, I'm just not in the mood anymore, that's all." I added, "Especially these days, I am very busy with my book. I have to do everything here, and at the same time, help Natatsha with her hairdressing business. I need to find money to publish my book."

He did not like my little explanation. To him, I should always be ready to satisfy his desires. But on my side, I had not forgotten what had happened in Haiti.

It was mid-August. My daughter felt that with the children at home, it was becoming difficult to run a hairdressing business there. She found a solution: buy a space or rent a chair in a salon so she could work outside the house.

August 12, 2000 journal

Natatsha bought her salon; she partnered with another hairdresser, each running her own business. She signed the papers this morning. She is proud. She deserves to be. I congratulated her because she works very hard. She is happy.

In the afternoon, I went with her to pick up the keys. I visited the salon. I think she made a good deal. I met her partner. She seems like a good person. They will work well together.

Back at my place, in the evening, I went upstairs to see her. She looked more relaxed. My question was direct: "So, how's it going?" Her response pleased me: "I feel like a boss and proud. I have my place, and I'm happy." She added this clarification: "This is just the beginning."

Part Two

An Experience on a Film Set

Or An Experience in Cinema

Towards the end of August, Natatsha got a contract on the set of an American film. She had been hired as a stylist. She asked for my help with fashion-related matters. We realized that a hairdresser was missing, so she was immediately hired as a hairdresser, and I worked as a stylist. I really enjoyed this experience. The lead actor was Erick Robert. I was responsible for remaking his clothes according to how he liked to wear them. I took his measurements with precision to reconstruct the outfit to his taste. I saw him very often. He was very kind and respectful to me. I also dressed other actors and actresses. I will never forget this experience.

Jacques, for his part, had found a job as a courier for banks (Dicom). He was doing quite well. But sometimes he asked me to accompany him to work. I agreed just to encourage him to keep the job. His schedule was relatively short: mornings from 5 a.m. to 8 a.m. and evenings from 9 p.m. to 11 p.m. I mostly accompanied him in the evenings when he went to pick up mail at Dorval Airport to deliver it to Place Bonaventure. These trips allowed me to walk around a bit. Once Jacques started making money, everything went well for him. He saved his salary to return to Haiti. He spent almost nothing on the apartment, only the bare essentials.

One day, we had a long discussion about returning to Haiti. He argued that we needed to save for this return. I kept repeating that I would never set foot in Haiti again. My priority was to ensure the publication of my book.

He said to me: "Well, my dear, I'm keeping my money to go back there! You'll manage." I immediately understood that he would not help me. I was well aware that he had saved a good amount. I asked him to lend me a portion. He laughed at me, saying: "You think I'm going to give you my money to invest in a book? You're wrong. Go elsewhere." At the moment, I didn't reply. I knew what to expect. To think that I had spent all the money from my inheritance to cover his reckless expenses in Haiti. From that day on, I no longer took for granted anything he told me.

The more money he earned, the more arrogant and vulgar he became toward me. He had resumed provoking unnecessary arguments. In short, he had fallen back into his detestable habits. In fact, he always acted this way when his wallet was full; he transformed into another character.

I let him be so as not to worsen the situation. But as the days went by, the more bitterness I felt toward him. He scrutinized all my actions.

On the sexual front, I did not oppose his fantasies. I no longer had the energy to fight with him. There were times when making love with him made me feel sick at heart, so little desire did I have for him.

It was December. I had become anxious and distressed. Here is what I wrote in my journal about it.

Journal – December 6, 2000

For the past few days, I don't know what's wrong with me especially today. I'm going around in circles in the apartment. Yet I have so many things to do. It's 11:30 in the morning. Jacques is still sleeping. I feel like a person waiting for something to happen, though I don't know what. I think it's anxiety.

The night before last, he was making love to me. When he penetrated me, something hurt deep inside. It was very painful. I couldn't take it. I felt that I really didn't want him anymore. But I made an effort so he wouldn't notice, because I dread his reaction whenever I admit that it hurts. Still, I ended up crying out, which displeased him. He dropped everything and used his usual irony, just to make me feel worse. He ridiculed me.

I truly came to believe that he was a sick man that he found pleasure in hurting his wife, a sadist. It seems he had done much harm to the young girl in Les Cayes. At least, that's what she told me before I left for Montreal. I think he misses all that. In the past, he inflicted so many sexual cruelties on me. Now, I no longer allow it. And he doesn't like that. He tries to manipulate me by suggesting that I'm starting to grow old, that I can no longer take part in rough physical games. And I reply: "Thanks for the compliment; that's exactly right." Let him do as he pleases I refuse to die before my time.

I'm not trying to feed hatred toward him. But deep inside, I know I don't love him anymore and that I will never live in Haiti with him again. For now, I'm focusing on my book, keeping a clear mind.

Part Three

Christmas in Montreal, in the Year 2000

During the month of December, I was extremely busy and went through many events. But I haven't yet had the chance to describe them. I'm entitled to a break, and I took advantage of a pause. I did, however, mention them in my journal. Here it is.

Journal – December 30, 2000

I was very busy during the month of December. Julie, my proofreader-editor, had given me seven transcribed copies of my manuscript. I distributed six of them to the reader-advisors, among them my son and my adoptive mother, Sister Berthe. I kept one copy for myself. I had to reread it and make some additions.

The advisors had one month to read my text and share their feedback. In the meantime, the Christmas season arrived. I went to lend a hand to my daughter at her hair salon. On Christmas Eve, I attended midnight mass at Saint Joseph's Oratory with Natatsha, Patrick, and their children. Jacques did not want to come. I enjoyed the ceremony. I felt good because it had been three years since I had last attended midnight mass at Christmas.

We celebrated with a family réveillon until 4:30 in the morning. The children opened their gifts. The scene reminded me of the time when my daughter and my son used to open their presents at home. On Christmas Day, I spent the time quietly at home with Jacques.

We had been invited to a party hosted by the Cayes Association. We did not go. I was too unwell with pain on my left side. So I chose instead to rest. Over the past few days, things had been going somewhat better with Jacques. But I still remained cautious.

On December 26, we went to Max's. We were all together, Natatsha being there with her little family. We spent a rather quiet New Year's. I went to see my sister and my brother to wish them a Happy New Year.

Jacques did not accompany me this time. When I returned, he looked at me as if trying to make me feel guilty. I pretended not to notice.

We enter the year 2001.

It is winter. The weather is cold. Although Jacques still suffers from pain in his injured arm, he keeps working anyway, because he has decided to leave for Haiti during the month of January. He figures he will spend at least part of the winter in the warmth. He plans to fly out on February 14, 2001, and intends to stay there for a month. That will do him good and me especially. I will have much more time to make the additions to my manuscript. Around February 10, my son-in-law fell ill, and Jacques had to replace him for a week. He had to work from 3 a.m. until 8 a.m. To encourage him, I kept him company. On top of that, he still worked his own evening shift. In reality, it was not too tiring, since during the day he did not work. He used that time to take care of his personal affairs.

When the time came for him to leave for Haiti, he asked his boss for a leave of absence. His boss refused. Jacques then claimed there had been a death in his family. The boss agreed to give him two weeks off. Yet Jacques had planned to stay a whole month. He went anyway.

Although he called to justify his absence, he was dismissed when he returned on March 17.

In the meantime, I was working intensely on my manuscript with the editor-corrector. We met once or twice a week. And I spent the weekend of March 12, 2001, at my sister's place. Here is what I wrote in my journal during that week.

Journal – March 12, 2001

I spent the weekend with my sister and my brother Robert. She and I went to the Home Show, and we had a very beautiful day. I enjoyed the weekend because I could see how happy my sister and brother were to have me with them. We talked about everything and nothing, but especially about Haiti.

Jacques is coming back from Haiti next week. Since we returned to Montreal, I have been trying to see whether our relationship can work with its ups and downs. During his absence, I was able to rest and go out a little, because I hardly had the time when he was at home.

I Continue My Story

My Daughter's Illness – 2001

At the beginning of March, Natatsha began having pain in her neck, which brought her to the hospital. At first, it was thought to be an infection. She had noticed a lump on the right side of her neck, and the doctors diagnosed lymph nodes. She spent a week recovering.

Just before her illness, she had gone through a tough work week. Her condition worried me a lot. Around March 28, I brought her back to the hospital. The specialist kept her in for surgery. He told me that he planned to do a biopsy to determine her condition. The operation lasted three hours. She was kept overnight in the hospital. In the meantime, I helped Patrick at home with the children. In the morning, he took them to daycare, and in the afternoon, I went to pick them up.

In the end, the biopsy revealed nothing in particular. The specialist wanted to carry out further tests because my daughter's neck kept swelling and she had a fever. Natatsha, meanwhile, was eager to leave. She only thought about getting back to work. "Your health comes first!" I advised her. She was going back and forth to the hospital. She became very weak. And I grew alarmed for her. I prayed to God to protect her because the children needed their mother. After a week, she looked like she was dying. The medical staff couldn't understand this illness, especially since all the tests had come back negative.

They went to get her birth records from the Notre-Dame Hospital to pursue the investigation further. Natatsha had told a doctor that she had been born anemic, that she had been hospitalized one month after birth because of a high fever, and that she had only been released after two months. They had therefore decided it was best to review her entire file.

One night, she had a dream in which my late father appeared. The next day, she felt well and no longer had a fever. The day after that, the doctors discharged her. Since that day, everything has been steady, but she keeps a close eye on her health.

Her illness had caused much sorrow for Patrick. He, like me, could no longer hide his sadness. We embraced, both wishing with all our hearts for her recovery. And Jesus answered us. She slowly regained her strength. We were happy she was back on her feet. I thank God a thousand times for it.

The Undertaken Initiatives

Natasha's state of health had delayed all her projects. The end of May was approaching. I resumed my activities. Natasha also went back to work. Now I was helping her much more often at her salon. At the same time, she and my son were working on the book's front cover.

She was beginning to prepare for the launch. We met with Julie to plan the steps to follow. I asked her to inquire about the possibility of my enrolling in a publishing course. The fact was that, in the meantime, I kept running into refusals from publishers who had no interest in publishing the autobiography of an unknown woman. I did indeed take the course. It gave me all the essential tools I needed to carry my project through.

Jacques, for his part, left again for Haiti on June 16, 2001. But, absorbed in my publishing efforts, I hardly even noticed his absence.

On the eve of June 24, 2001, Natasha and Patrick, and the children left for the countryside for a three-day stay. I went instead to my sister's. I also found myself closer to Saint-Jean-Baptiste Church on Rachel Street, near Saint-Denis. My sister, I should mention, lives nearby, on Mentana Street. I was happy to live and share a faith in such a family way.

My stay with Irène turned out to be very pleasant. By the way, I would like to recount the following anecdote. One day, my sister noticed a ladybug on one of the trees in her yard. We had never imagined an insect of that size. It was yellow with black spots. I immediately advised my sister to inform the city so that someone would come to collect it, which they did. But the municipal workers were also astonished at the size of the insect, so much so that they planned to have it examined in a laboratory. A truly disturbing and most mysterious incident. For me, it remains a mystery. I thought about it all evening.

Taking Care of My Grandson

This evening, I am at Max and Yole's. I came to look after my grandson Isaiah, since his parents had to be away to attend the wedding of one of Yole's sisters.

I arrived at my son's house at 4:15 p.m. Isaiah was napping. When he woke up at 6:30, I served him his supper. Around 8:00, I gave him his bath and put him to bed. I sang to him, which he really enjoyed. During the evening, he and I played a little. He is naturally very calm. He is a sweet little boy. He didn't cry at all during the evening. As for me, I was very happy to spend this time with my grandson, because I am always with Natasha's children. I need to get to know him as well.

I don't know if I will stay overnight here. It will depend on the time they return. But I would rather sleep in my own bed. We'll see.

Journal – July 9, 2001

Today I went shopping downtown with my sister. We had arranged to meet at the McGill metro station. We went to La Baie to buy Fashion Fair beauty products and some clothes, because I was invited to a wedding on July 14, that of one of Natasha's childhood friends. We didn't linger at La Baie, since our friend Dédé had promised to visit my sister.

As soon as we got back, we began preparing a simple dinner: rice and Lima beans with grilled chicken ordered from the Portuguese place. We also made a good salad.

When Dédé arrived, he had dinner with us and with my brother. My sister, Dédé, and I ended up getting completely drunk! We polished off three bottles of wine. I was tipsy. We talked about everything and nothing. When I got up, I staggered around it was funny to see. We laughed so much, and it did us good.

That night, I stayed over at my sister's. The next day, Saturday, I went back home. As soon as I arrived, the phone rang. It was Jacques calling me from Haiti to give me his news. I told him a little about what I had been up to. He talked about the heat there, the high cost of living, and so on.

The following Sunday, I went on an outing to Saint-Sauveur with Natasha, Patrick, and their children. We did some shopping. But I also fulfilled a dream I had cherished since 1970 in New York: riding in a horse-drawn carriage. My son-in-law treated us to a ride. Yes, indeed! Our little family rode in a carriage through the streets of Saint-Sauveur.

The children were delighted and excited. I was over the moon. I thanked Patrick with these words: *"You've made one of my dreams come true."* My confession made him happy. We went back home glowing with joy.

We quickly prepared supper. During the meal, we were all lively and enchanted by our day. I had an exceptional weekend.

July 20, 2001

Natasha and Patrick Go on a Trip – I Look After the Children

Today is Friday. I woke up at 8 this morning with Natasha and Patrick's two little children in the same bed as me. It was pure happiness.

Natasha and Patrick left yesterday, July 19, for Cuba. They'll be away for a week. I drove them to the airport yesterday at noon, along with the children. Our hearts were heavy. But I know they're doing it for their own good especially Natasha, who really needs rest. The young parents felt a little sad too, since it's the first time they've been separated from their children. On the way back from the airport, the children asked me many questions. Elle-Camay confided to me that she was going to pray to little Jesus so that bad people wouldn't hurt her parents.

Afterward, we went to my sister's. From there, I took the children to Lafontaine Park nearby to cheer them up. Elle-Camay wanted to go to her favorite store, the Dollar Store. I promised her that we'd go tomorrow.

When we got back home, after putting each of them to bed in their own rooms, I went downstairs to fetch my pillows because I would be sleeping in my daughter's room. I couldn't leave the children alone upstairs. I was the only one with them, since Jacques was still in Haiti.

We had a good night. Mikaël had a nightmare. Around 2 a.m., he came to lie down beside me. He told me he couldn't sleep. He spoke about his house and about his daddy. I whispered to him, *"You need to sleep if you want everything to go well for them over there."* I managed to comfort him, and he fell asleep.

Around 6 a.m., Elle-Camay came to join us in bed. She still had sleep in her eyes. At 8:30, we were all awake. We had breakfast together. Then we made the bed and tidied up the room. I washed them and got them dressed. Around 10:30, I called my son Max, and he invited us over. We would also take the opportunity to go to the pool with his son. Elle-Camay and Mikaël were overjoyed when they heard the news.

Journal

At the park near Max's place

I am at the park next to Max's house on Sherbrooke Street West, at the corner of Park Row East. The children, Max, and Yole are swimming in the pool. I am sitting on the ground under a tree, writing. I watch them, and I see the joy they feel being together.

I rejoice for them, and I thank Jesus for giving me the chance to see my grandchildren and, above all, to witness their happiness at being with me. I feel fulfilled. It is a treasure. They are my loves the children and their parents. I love them very much. It is because of them that I want to write my life story, to leave them a memory and to help them avoid repeating my mistakes.

We had supper at Max's. We spent a wonderful day, and everyone was full of joy.

I continue my story

During Natatsha and Patrick's absence, I had much to do with the children. I needed to rest before resuming my personal activities. All the more so since, in September, I was starting my course on publishing. It was the end of July. I planned to take my vacation before Jacques's return in August. Otherwise, I would never find time to rest.

I spoke about it to Natatsha. I told her that I would go to New York on July 19 for a week. I made the decision without telling Jacques, because he certainly would have forbidden me from taking the trip.

In my journal, I described how the trip unfolded as well as my stay in New York.

Journal – July 29, 2001

The Trip

It is 2:30 p.m. I am on a Rabaud coach bus headed to New York. I am going for a one-week stay. It is the first time I have traveled on this bus line. Usually, I make the trip by car or on a Greyhound. It had been three years since I last went to New York. In the past, I would go very often with Jacques and the children when they were young.

I love traveling by plane, by car, or by bus. I used to travel at least three or four times a year, sometimes even more. But for the past year, since my return from Haiti, I had stopped. I needed that break in order to stabilize myself, focus on me, and concentrate on my book.

Jacques always claimed we couldn't go to New York because he needed money to return to Haiti. But I had money, and his excuse didn't hold up. This time, I made up my mind and did what I thought was best for me. I know that when he returns, things won't be the same. I prepared myself for that.

We arrived at the Canadian–American border, at the duty-free store. The driver and his assistant gave us 15 minutes to shop or go to the bathroom. I stayed in the bus.

The driver pulled out without bothering to count the passengers. He had forgotten a woman and two children. Luckily, there was another bus. They managed to catch up with us at the immigration checkpoint.

At the checkpoint, everyone had to get off the bus for the U.S. immigration inspection. I went to the bathroom for two minutes.

When I came back, the bus was gone! The driver had left me at the border. Another bus was waiting for its passengers. I went up to the driver and asked, "Where is the bus that was here?" He replied, "It left. If you want, come with me. I'll catch up to it in Baltimore." I accepted his offer and sat down in the bus.

I was worried about losing my suitcase, which was in the first bus. "What will happen," I thought, "if we can't catch up to it in Baltimore? That one was going to Brooklyn, and I was headed to Queens." The first driver was a short man, of Haitian origin, speaking both Creole and English. He was extremely arrogant. Most of the passengers found his behavior unprofessional. The second driver, in contrast, was a Québécois, what they call *pure laine* genuinely kind and considerate. He was flexible and patient with the travelers, especially the elderly and the children, who kept running back and forth to the bathroom.

The continuation

It is 6:00 p.m.; I am still on the road to New York. I am not sleeping. I do a bit of reading and observe the actions of the passengers. From time to time I look at the landscape. I have a lot on my mind; I will take advantage of the trip to write.

Since Jacques left for Haiti, the times I have spent with my children and grandchildren have changed me a great deal. I have become calmer, more thoughtful. I think a lot about myself and about how to live my life. I help my daughter a little at her hair salon. I meet other people, and I have grown closer to my sister. Despite everything, I admit that I still think of Jacques not as before, however, and I pray a lot to learn how to live alone; Jacques was often absent, and I was very busy with the launch of my book. I must learn to tame my solitude.

In fact, I do not like being alone, and I am looking for an alternative. I will need to examine carefully this constraining side of my character and pray that God lend me aid.

Let's return to the account of the trip

Upon arriving in Baltimore, I found the first bus. I got back on after thanking the driver who had helped me out. Even though I was hungry, I didn't dare get off the bus to go buy something to eat; I feared that the Haitian driver would forget me once again. A gentleman of a certain age sitting next to me gave me a sandwich and a bottle of water. So it was thanks to him that I was able to have a little food. I then remembered that my sister Irène had advised me not to travel with the Rabeau buses. But I had ignored her warning.

When I got back on the bus, I didn't reproach the driver for having left me behind at the border. Above all, I didn't want to have any more problems with him. He was very grumpy. But in the end, everything turned out fine. And I truly enjoyed my trip.

Journal – August 3, 2001

My Stay in New York

It is noon, I am alone in Queens (Rosedale) at Addely's place. Her sister Dedzye brought me here to wait until my departure for Montreal. I could no longer stay at Aunt Dadia's because she was invited to a charismatic conference and her youngest daughter was returning to work. So I would spend these few hours at my cousin's until my departure for Montreal at 9 p.m. I am taking advantage of this free moment to recount my stay at Aunt Dadia's in New York.

It was a very pleasant week. Upon my arrival on the evening of Sunday, July 29, I said this prayer: *"Jesus, thank you for the trip; also, I beg you, make my stay go well."* It had been four years since I had last seen Aunt Dadia, her two daughters, and her son Claudy.

As in previous years, she gave me her bedroom entirely at my disposal. I would sleep there alone, she had decided. After my short prayer, I immediately fell asleep because the trip had exhausted me. I had a good night's sleep. I got up at 7 a.m. as it had been planned that I would accompany Aunt Dadia to church, with Mass scheduled for 8:30 in the morning.

After getting out of bed, I got ready and we left. I was delighted to see her again at her home. She hadn't changed. Even the house was the same. With one difference, the kitchen and the bathrooms had been renovated.

It is always a joy for me to go to Saint-Rose-of-Lima Church because, during the week, Mass is held in the small chapel and there is exposition of the Blessed Sacrament before and after Mass.

During my five days in New York, I went to Mass every morning with Aunt Dadia. We then stayed an hour for adoration. At home, we recited the Chaplet of Divine Mercy every day at 3 p.m. These moments did me good. We spent one day at her eldest daughter Addely's house, as we were waiting for the delivery of a package for her and her husband, since they could not be absent from work.

I should add that at that time, Addely was pregnant. To help her a little, we did a thorough cleaning of the house. Once the cleaning was done, we sat in the living room to chat and watch television. We spoke of our joys and sorrows of the past, especially hers, since Aunt Dadia was separated from her husband. We laughed, cried, and prayed. It felt good to let go a little.

On Tuesday, July 31, Jacques called me from Haiti. It was Aunt Dadia who answered. He spoke rudely to her. When she handed me the phone, I calmly greeted Jacques. He shouted insults at me. He was very angry about my trip to New York. He snapped: *"You went to New York while I'm in Haiti. I need money to go to Les Cayes. I hope you didn't use my money for your crazy trip."* I told him that I had entrusted his money to Natatsha. I would ask her to send him a transfer. I wanted to know the address to send the money to. He kept cackling without stopping, to the point where I couldn't get a word in. At some point, his calling card expired. I asked my daughter to send him a transfer to Port-au-Prince. That matter was now settled. Jacques is a very insolent man. I never touch his money, and I never ask him for any either.

He did not call me back; that is indirect proof that he had received the money. I know he is supposed to return from Haiti on August 11. I am not looking forward to his return because physically and morally, I am not ready. But what can you do!

Aunt Dadia had invited a friend to spend a few days at her place. The day before her arrival, we cleaned everything thoroughly to welcome her well. We also did a complete grocery run. At the end of the day, we were completely exhausted.

I truly don't know where Aunt Dadia finds all this energy at her age. She is 67, but she looks 50. Watching her in full action, one might even think she is only 25 or 30. I'll stop writing for now Addely and her husband are back from work.

Chapter 13

I Return to Montreal

Everything went well during my return trip to Montreal. This time, the driver was extremely proper; he knew his job very well. I had gone to New York with the intention of resting, but in the end, I did not rest. Still, it did me good to make this trip. I was able to see members of my family, which pleased them greatly. I also enjoyed a different environment that truly lifted my spirits.

As soon as I returned to Montreal, I felt as if everything was going wrong. I still felt tired. Jacques had returned on August 11. I didn't have a single minute for myself. I couldn't understand why I saw everything so differently.

Here is what I wrote under these circumstances on August 28.

August 28, 2001

It is 3:30 a.m., I cannot sleep. Everything is boiling in my head. My husband Jacques came back very thin and worn out from Haiti. He continues to work and to wear himself down. And he is always in a bad mood.

He doesn't listen to my advice. My daughter Natatsha also never stops working, even though she is sick. Her husband works just a little; he hasn't found a job yet. Little Elle-Camay starts school this morning. The children are not yet baptized. And then there is Max, whose wife is pregnant and who constantly complains of fatigue. She laments that her little boy doesn't sleep during the day. And finally, my own situation: I need financing for my book. I don't know who to turn to; yet, I sense that someone will help me. I just don't know how to approach them. I am already thinking about the future reactions of readers once they have read my book, about the positive or negative criticism, etc. I feel like my head is going to explode. I pray to God to help me.

Sometimes, I feel like canceling everything. A few minutes later, I reason with myself: *"No, Enice, don't do that. This is important. It is a dream you have always wanted to fulfill, and you yourself have said that you want this book to help people. So don't give up."* But apart from my children, Sister Berthe, my brother Villard, and Patrick, I did not receive much support. My friends, listeners, and acquaintances did not take me seriously. Even Jacques did not encourage me much. I was sad and weary.

Besides, since my return from New York, I no longer had the desire to write. I felt too depressed to do so. On top of that, I was disturbed by Jacques's presence. I no longer had a minute to myself. I constantly had to take care of him. Above all, he never missed his dose of vitamins in the evening, and sometimes in the morning: sex. Even if I was not willing, he helped himself anyway. Sex had become his favorite toy.

Well, I will try to get some sleep because I must wake up at 6:30 to prepare breakfast and lunch for Jacques.

I continue my story

In the meantime, life goes on. It is now September 2001. I am resuming my activities regarding my book. I am supposed to start my publishing course this month. I am eager, because I have much to learn for the publication. I am also looking for a good proofreader for the final revision of the work. I am soon finishing the writing of the epilogue and the preface.

On September 11, 2001, I was in the kitchen with Jacques. We were having breakfast and watching television at the same time. Suddenly, I see a plane crashing into a skyscraper: *"Look, something is happening on television,"* I said to Jacques. He replied: *"You saw it too." I continued: *"Maybe it's a scene from a new movie."* At that very moment, I heard on the news that a plane had just crashed into a building, one of the towers in Manhattan. A few minutes later, a second plane.

That day, I suspended all my activities. I had a bad day. I thought about the people inside the towers and their families. It was a very dark day. I will never forget it.

I attended my course during the month of October. I had no time to write. I was too busy.

One fine day, a friend recommended a proofreader. Natatsha and I went to bring him the manuscript. He agreed to join us. He has a lot of experience in the field. He started the revision around October 30. Rereading the manuscript, I find that he has done a good job.

But since I embarked on this adventure, it is the first time I feel a real unease. I don't know why. Yet, I have the situation well in hand. Everything will go well. My daughter noticed my hesitation. She knows me very well. I reassured her that things would work out. I will pray for this intention.

Journal   November 22, 2001

Last night, I had a terrible nightmare. When I woke up, I found myself at the foot of the bed. For some time now, I feel like I am in a period of transition. I don't even understand myself.

Jacques was supposed to leave for Haiti two weeks ago. In the end, he is leaving Monday, November 27, passing through New York. He is taking the bus to get to New York. He is happy to go to Haiti. He swears that he feels good there. Good for him.

Memory

During the year 2001, Jacques returned to Haiti three times. I have come to terms with having a part-time husband. I am now used to his absences. I am beginning to learn how to live on my own. Besides, I no longer have the time to feel lonely. At the beginning, it was difficult. Gradually, I am getting used to it.

Journal December 13, 2001

I am at the Café Bistro located at the corner of Rachel and Saint-Laurent. It is 11:50. I am waiting for Julie, my copy editor. Our meeting was scheduled for 11:00. She has not yet arrived. I will wait until 12:15. If I don't see her, I will leave. For now, I continue writing.

Since Jacques left for Haiti, he has called me only once. I don't know how things are going for him. No news is good news. For me, everything is going well at the moment. I have many steps to take for the book. I don't have time to feel lonely.

I am also continuing to work a lot on my temperament. I want to keep a positive mindset, be less emotional, more patient, and wiser. I think I am beginning to make progress. I pray with this intention. I look at myself in the mirror and I see another woman, stronger and more self-assured.

I spoke with Sister Berthe this week. She was happy to have news from me and to learn that I found a good proofreader for the book. This man gives me very wise advice. He has become a friend.

I had lunch yesterday with my sister at a restaurant on Saint-Denis Street. We talked about everything and nothing, except my book. She is very kind and good to me, but she doesn't encourage me morally about the book. She gives the impression of someone who wouldn't like the book to be published. Yet, I haven't written anything bad about anyone in my family in the book. I only told my truth.

It is noon, I am still at the Café Bistro and Julie has not yet arrived. I'll wait ten more minutes; if I don't see her, I'll leave. She can come meet me at my daughter's salon. It's not such a big deal. To pass the time, I continue writing in my journal. I must learn to be more patient. I will call her house and leave a message.

Present Moment   March 2, 2007

Last Night

Hello, my little ones, I haven't spoken to you for quite some time. I couldn't do it because I wanted to make progress on my book. Today is March 2, 2007. I am almost at the end. See you soon!

My story has now reached December 2001. I still have to recount the year 2002, which will not be long, and the first five months of 2003. I am happy to see that you are still here with me to continue my mysterious adventures. You encourage me a lot, and I thank you for your support. I would like you to pray to God for me, to ask Him to give me health, energy, and strength to carry my journey to the end. Because last night, I was not feeling well. I was terribly tired. I couldn't write. I had to go to bed. I had a strong pain in my chest, in one arm, and in my back. I eventually fell asleep without even turning off my bedside lamp. It was 9 p.m. Around midnight, I woke up. I had palpitations.

I didn't call my loved ones; I didn't want to disturb them. I hoped it would be temporary. I was afraid, though. I got up. I went to the living room. I turned on the computer and started looking at pictures to relax, as I usually do. But I didn't feel any better. I was really unwell.

I remembered that I had my supply of pills. Despite my doctor's warnings, I took half of a sleeping pill. After that, I went back to bed. I stayed calm until sleep carried me away. I woke up around 9:30 in the morning. It did me good. I feel better today. No, no, I will not abandon you at all.

We are approaching the end of my story. I must see it through to the end. Wish me good luck and courage. I love you very much, my darlings.

I Continue My Story

Part One

The Year 2001 ends

At the close of this year, I don't feel like celebrating. It isn't because I am sad, no. It's because I am deeply preoccupied. My mind is entirely focused on the release of my book. I must not make mistakes. I am the only one overseeing everything. My daughter, for her part, is taking care of the launch itself: choosing a hall, arranging the buffet, managing publicity, and the presentations. She and my son worked on the front and back covers. I, meanwhile, watched over everything that concerned the book's publication. It was precisely for this purpose that I had taken my course.

Jacques, on the other hand, managed to be absent at the very moment I needed him most. He flatly refused to help me financially, morally, or materially. He was supposed to return from Haiti on December 26. He called me to say he had changed his plans. He would only return in February. So, I no longer counted on him. I had to prepare myself to erase him from my mind for a time, in order to remain mentally strong.

This Christmas passed very quietly for me. The children, as well as my sister, spoiled me a great deal. On the eve of the holidays, I worked at my daughter's salon because I needed money for the book's publication. By December 28, the layout was finished. All that remained was for the proofreader to do one last check of the manuscript.

In the meantime, I was already thinking about the second volume of the book. Before beginning it, I would have to focus on just one critic and remove many psychological obstacles. To achieve this, I needed to recover my peace of mind and heart. I would have to return far into my memories. I anticipated that this inner journey would be difficult, painful, even terrifying! But by then, it had become a certainty: I had to do it.

I remember that when Jacques called me to warn me he would not be coming back, I thought that perhaps it was better that way. He does what he loves, and I, too do what I love, and what soothes my being. Yet every time the memory of all the harm he has caused me comes back, I ask myself why I don't leave him. Still, I cannot find the answer to that question. My daughter, when I spoke to her about it, gave me this advice: *"Mammy, you must think with your heart."* One of my friends, with whom I also discussed it, expressed her perplexity this way: *"As soon as you find the answer to your question, let me know."* This is what, in those moments, I wrote in my journal about Jacques.

Journal December 29, 2001

These days, I don't know what is happening inside me. It feels as though one part of me wants nothing to do with him, while another part remains deeply sensitive toward him. That same part of me no longer needs him, neither financially nor emotionally. It only needs to talk to him. But it is clear that communication is impossible. When he speaks, it is only to provoke arguments. Often, he treats her with contempt. But fortunately, she has changed. She is no longer so vulnerable.

But, good Lord, why can't she finally make a decision? As for me, every time I think about it, it hurts. It hurts because I've realized that I cannot make any decision at all. In short, I don't know what to do. I will call Sister Berthe, my adoptive mother. Surely, she will be able to help me. I will ask her for an appointment.

I Continue My Story

My daughter and I share the goal of holding the book launch at the beginning of spring, that is, in two months, since today is December 31. We will have to double our efforts to be completely ready.

We are still working to gather the money required for printing the book. My optimism about this is unwavering. My son-in-law, however, has his doubts, which he expressed to me kindly: *"Now that your book is finished, what will you do if you don't have enough money for the printing?"*

I immediately replied: *"I'm not worried. I will find the money in time, and the launch will take place as planned on March 14, 2002."*

He smiled approvingly: *"You really do have such a positive spirit. Bravo, dear Enice!"* Then he kissed me. That sign of trust truly warmed my heart. I was also proud of my attitude direct and positive at the same time.

Chapter 14

The Beginning of 2002

The Year of the Launch of A Woman Among So Many Others

I spent New Year's Day and the following day at my sister Irène's, where my brother Robert also lives. Being together fills us with joy.

After the holiday season and New Year celebrations, activities resumed. Natatsha was working less, as it was the slow season in hairdressing. This allowed her to devote more time to organizing the launch of my book.

To prepare for the event, we set up a very dedicated team. Natatsha and Max designed the invitation cards themselves, with the help of their friend Stephan, who handled the graphic design. All the operations were well planned. Natatsha had reserved a hall even before the holiday season. She was constantly assisted by the young Québécois writer J.L. My son-in-law, meanwhile, managed the website.

Even though I took part in supervising the entire operation, I continued to help my children with their little ones. At the same time, I made it a duty to take care of myself, both spiritually and physically. Here is an excerpt from my journal.

January 16, 2002

I have had no news from Jacques since January. I called Les Cayes, and his nephew assured me that he was in Port-au-Prince. I am supposed to meet Lionel, my proofreader, this afternoon to give him a document. Over the phone, he mentioned that from the sound of my voice, he could tell I was tired. I explained that I had slept poorly the night before. He advised me to rest.

Following his advice, I went to bed a little earlier. The next day, I already felt much better. He seems to worry about me, though I don't know why. When he called me back, he was glad to hear that I was doing better.

January 29, 2002

Yesterday, I received from Stephan the first draft of the book cover. I was moved as I examined it; Stephan had done a very good job. I kissed him to thank him. He deserved that "little kiss," even if I was paying him for his work. I also admire the active participation of my two children, whom I have not yet thanked. Above all, they were the ones who came up with the idea for the design. I congratulate them.

When I arrived home last night, I prayed. I thanked God for everything He has given me. I placed the mockup of the cover page on my little prayer table. And I fell asleep right away, it was midnight. (End of the journal).

February 1, 2002

My friend Nelia arrived from Haiti. She will be staying in Montreal for a month. Yesterday, I went to pick her up so she could spend a day at my house. It was snowing, it was cold, and the roads were slippery. I had errands to run, and I took her along with me. The streets were icy, so I drove carefully to avoid skidding off the road or getting into an accident. I was actually going to Verdun to pick up the book cover.

The next day, I had an appointment with the printer. Thankfully, everything went well. Back home, we settled in the kitchen to chat. Since it had been such a long time since we had last seen each other, we had much to catch up on. When it came time to prepare dinner, I offered her the first pages of my book along with the back cover to read.

She began reading quietly, silently. Meanwhile, I busied myself with the dinner preparations. After a few minutes, I turned my head toward her. She had tears in her eyes. With an emotional voice, she simply said to me, *"You know, I won't continue reading today. You'll send me a copy of your book in Haiti. I'll read it there. Today, I don't feel ready to read it."* Then she added, *"During all the time I used to see you writing in Haiti, I didn't realize you were writing your life story. I congratulate you, dear, you did well. This was important for you. Bravo again."* I thanked her with a kiss.

After dinner, I took her to do her personal shopping. All in all, we had a very good day. I keep a pleasant memory of those beautiful moments shared with her. It was tender and sincere.

Chapter 15

Part One

Preparing for the Launch

I remember very clearly the day I went to pick up my fully completed book. I was radiant and confident. It was my baby, sitting right next to me in the car. It felt just like when I had my two children. I had fought for its birth, just as I had fought for theirs. And now it was here or almost; only the printing remained. I spoke to it in the car, reassuring it: *"Don't worry, I will find the money to bring you into the world. I know you will be able to help the people who need you, but still, I feel a little sad to let you go on your way."*

I was overjoyed. I prayed to God to keep me under His protection. I thought of my sister and called her on my cell phone to see if she was back from work. I told her I would drop by. When I arrived, I stepped out of the car with my manuscript in my hands. My brother was there as well.

We went into the kitchen before dinner. Showing them my work, I said: *"Here it is, my book, my third baby. All that's left is the printing. I'm missing a bit of money to get it done, but I'm sure I'll find it, even if it takes some time. At least, the book itself is finished."*

At first, they remained silent. I watched closely for their reactions to the fruit of my constant effort. My brother had a smile on his face, the kind of smile he shows when he is truly pleased. My sister, without a doubt, was happy for my success, but nothing in her attitude showed it. After dinner, I left, but before going home, I stopped at my daughter's salon to check that everything was going well.

Back at home, I received a call from my sister inviting me to her place the following afternoon. She told me that she, our brother, and one of our friends had gathered a certain amount of money for me. I was delighted by such encouraging news. And that wasn't all two other friends also offered me generous loans, as did Madame Bélisle. In just two days, I had collected all the money I needed.

For me, it was a true miracle. God had answered my prayers. Once the book launch was over, I had a Mass of thanksgiving celebrated. I then gave thanks to my sister Irène, my brother Robert, as well as to the friends who believed in me and in my project. Finally, I expressed my gratitude to my two beloved children, to my son-in-law who had always supported me, and to all my loved ones. But I must emphasize the contribution of my daughter, who continues to help me both morally and spiritually in the writing of my second book: *"She is my psychologist."*

Part Two

The Book Launch

In the days leading up to it, I had to endure an overload of work: multiple revisions of my presentation speech, several dress rehearsals to choose my outfit, and more. I felt swollen with fatigue and stress. My sister had ordered a generous buffet. Natatsha decorated the hall with her friend J.L., and Patrick, my son-in-law, was the host of the event. Due to a traffic incident, I arrived at the launch venue a few minutes late. All the guests were already there, waiting for me.

In a rush and pressed for time, Natatsha helped me get ready. I quickly went up on stage. Patrick introduced me. The room was packed. I was moved to see that so many people had come to share this moment with us.

That evening, I felt calm and composed. By the time I stepped onto the stage, all my worries and stress had melted away. I felt at ease. I was able to read my message slowly and clearly. I could sense that people were listening with great attention. I was filled with a strength of serenity and true happiness. My heart was joyful. It was my night! For the first time, I was thinking only of myself.

A little later, I went from table to table to greet each guest individually. My adoptive mother was there with Sister Rachel, Madame Bélisle with one of her daughters, my sister with her friends, my son's friends, the singer Natacha, as well as the whole team who had worked on the book, including Lionel, Julie, Aunt Dadia, and many other warm-hearted people.

The hall was beautifully decorated, with eggshell and red tablecloths spread across the tables. During the signing session, the host introduced the guests. Julie read the prologue, Natatsha shared details about the book, the publishing house, and the editorial team. Words of thanks were also expressed by Natatsha and Max.

The book launch was a resounding success. I received numerous testimonies from women thanking me for having written it. They held my hand as a sign of their gratitude. For me, it was a great source of pride. And I joyfully signed the dedications. The people were in high spirits it showed on their faces.

Throughout the evening, a young photographer captured faces and took group photos. A friend of Max filmed the event. Even today, when I watch the tape, I can hardly believe the joy I brought to my guests that night. I will never forget it. All of this was possible thanks to my faith in the divine, in myself, and in my daughter and son.

Aunt Dadia had come from New York to attend the launch. I drove her to my sister's house afterward. My plan was to then return home and sleep alone, since Jacques had not returned from Haiti for the launch.

Our friend, the psychologist P.N., advised my sister not to let me drive back. He remarked, *"She's not doing well, don't let her leave in this state."* So, I agreed to spend the night at my sister's.

Settling into the living room, I sat on the corner of the sofa. Suddenly, I felt overwhelmed with sadness. I was in great pain. I did not speak. I stared into nothingness. When it was time to go to bed, my sister settled us into her room. Aunt Dadia fell asleep quickly, but I could not. I was too sad, too hurt. I could no longer hold it in. I cried out and wept bitterly.

My sister came into the room, wanting to know what was wrong. I couldn't explain it. My suffering was too deep. My whole body hurt my stomach twisted as if I had a knot in my heart. I thought about my book, about my readers. It was as if I had lost a child, not knowing if it would truly accomplish what I hoped it would.

At last, I opened up a little. She brought me into the kitchen and comforted me with her words. As dawn broke, she made coffee. We had breakfast with Aunt Dadia. Around 8 a.m., I returned home. I needed to be alone to gather my thoughts.

Here is what I wrote five days after the book launch.

March 19, 2002

Before the launch, I couldn't write. My mind was too preoccupied. Now that everything is over, I still can't manage it. And yet, everything is in my head. I'm living through the event in silence. It's as if I wanted to keep it entirely to myself.

I still feel sad. I don't know why. I shut myself away at home. Yet, I must get moving, since it's up to me to make the arrangements to place the books in bookstores and libraries. Natatsha had taken care of promotion with the media. I need to get back on track, I must.

I continue my story

Jacques called me from Haiti to ask that I send him a plane ticket since his return ticket had expired. As for the money, he didn't hesitate to say to me: *"You just had your launch, you have money, you can buy the ticket."*

I replied: *"It's true that I sold some books, but I cannot buy your plane ticket. I need that money to pay, among other things, my collaborators. But there's another reason: you deliberately chose not to come to my launch, an event that was very important to me. So call your cousin or someone else. She'll buy it for you."*

Here is what I wrote in my diary.

The Return of Jacques

Friday, March 29, 2002

I am on a bus heading to Trois-Rivières. I am going on a pilgrimage to Cap-de-la-Madeleine with my sister Irène and our friend Lucie. I will take advantage of the trip to write. Jacques came back yesterday; I went to pick him up at 5:15 p.m.

When we met, I kissed him on the cheek, as one would a friend. I did this without really thinking. I forgot that he was my husband. On the drive home, I was the one driving the car. I could feel he was nervous. We talked about everything and nothing.

As soon as we arrived home, he asked me if I still loved him. "Why?" I replied. He answered: *"I don't know, I noticed that you kissed me on the cheek."* I tried to explain: *"You know, I didn't do it on purpose, I just thought you had become like a friend or a brother because you've been away for so long. And after everything that has happened, I don't know anymore."* He wanted to talk. *"Not right now,"* I objected. *"I'm expecting Lionel, who is coming to pick up some books for his friends. We'll talk after."*

When Lionel arrived, the children called me. I went upstairs to meet him. The children went to greet their grandfather. They were happy to see him. Jacques greeted Lionel by shaking his hand. He thanked him for helping me with the book. I was watching Lionel's reaction. He looked at Jacques with a mischievous glance, as if he wanted to say a lot, but he made no comment.

Lionel and I sat down in the dining room. He stayed for about 30 minutes. Whenever he visits, he always tells me stories to make me laugh.

As soon as he left, I went downstairs to find Jacques. He was already in bed, reading the book. I sat down next to him, half-seated on the bed. I immediately started the conversation: *"I want you to listen. I'm the one who's going to speak, and I don't want you to interrupt me. You'll give me your answer afterward."*

He then explained that he hadn't come to the book launch because he felt excluded from every event, that he was always unnecessary. Right away, I recognized these as excuses. I objected, telling him he was distorting the truth, that he had excluded himself from everything. On top of that, he refused to lend me money whenever he had some. Still, he went on inventing justifications. It was a lost cause.

He went on with the conversation, referring to the book:

"You never told me about this unknown lover you mentioned in your autobiography, why?"

I replied: *"You know, Jacques, almost all women have a secret garden in their hearts; they always keep an intimate corner that helps them get through gloomy days."*

"During all the time you were sleeping beside me," he continued, *"were you dreaming of that secret lover?"*

I shot back: "I made it very clear in the book that it happened mostly when I was sad, and I regret nothing."

He pressed me to reveal the name of the person. "Never," was my reply. "You forget that it's me, Jacques, you're talking to. What's going on? So you don't love me?"

He kept insisting, asking the same questions. Holding the book in his hands, he threw at me: "The love you described in the book, do you still feel that for me?"

My response was blunt: "Honestly, I don't anymore. Since the day you brought another woman into my bed, to sleep with her, that love vanished and forever."

I added: "In order to be able to write that part of the book, I had to step back into my 20-year-old self, and start making love to you again as I did back then. You know, it was very hard for me at that time; I suffered a lot."

Hearing me describe something so painful, he started to cry, to my great surprise. I didn't react, wanting to hide my own emotion. What he didn't suspect was that, during his comings and goings in Haiti, my book had taken his place.

He swore to me that he still loved me, just like before. And he went on to insist: *"All the girls I went to see meant nothing to me."*

After the launch, I gradually resumed my activities. The book was well received by the bookstores. A week after the launch, I began receiving very positive comments by email, by postal mail, and by phone.

These signs of great interest gave me a new burst of energy. That year, I took part in book-signing sessions in several bookstores. In November, I participated in the Montreal Book Fair. I then went to New York, also for book signings, as well as to different book fairs in Quebec, etc. During the quiet moments of my signing sessions, I would return to my journal.

Some parts of my journal during my book-signing sessions I always find some quiet time to write.

Journal   May 11, 2002

I am at the Ruffin bookstore located in the Rive-Nord shopping center in Repentigny for a book-signing session. It is 12:30 p.m. They have set me up right in front of the store entrance. I am sitting next to a round table covered with a yellow tablecloth, holding a pile of copies of *Une femme parmi tant d'autres*. To make the table more attractive, I placed a small pot of roses, a little candle, and some crescent-shaped bookmarks. I arranged the books with care to catch the readers' eyes. I do this at every signing session.

It was the day before Mother's Day, so the mall was crowded. People walked by and glanced over. Some stopped to look at the book. Others asked me how long I had been writing and why I had decided to write. Over time, I realized that, everywhere I go, people ask me the same questions. Many curious readers read the back cover. Very young girls also asked me questions.

Ah! Someone just bought a copy, and I quickly dedicate it. Then others follow suit. Ah! A young girl just bought one for her mother-in-law! Other passersby stop and do the same. Ah! This little girl is getting one for her mom, and so on.

During this signing session, the mother of my son-in-law, Patrick came by to encourage me. After greeting me, she went to sit on a nearby bench by the bookstore. A fellow from Miragoâne, Michel, brought me a beautiful bouquet of flowers. His gesture gave me great joy.

The session, which ended at 4 p.m., lasted two hours. The sales were very successful. I was very satisfied, and so were the bookstore staff. The most important thing was to make the book known. Usually, after a successful sale, something good follows. Jacques came to pick me up after dropping Patrick's mother off at her place. My friend Michel, who lives in Repentigny, invited us over to his home.

June 2, 2002

I haven't written in several days because I've been very busy. I have books to send, among other places, to New York and Miami. In fact, I find myself managing more than one matter at the same time: keeping the house in order, work at Natatsha's salon, and taking daily care of Jacques. There are also radio interviews, ongoing book-signing sessions, and long phone conversations.

Jacques multiplies his fits of jealousy and goes through my personal belongings, hoping to discover I don't know what. He even flies into a rage when, during radio interviews, I'm asked questions about certain topics addressed in the book. He claims not to understand why I felt stifled and suffocated, even though he almost constantly tried to hinder my writing work.

June 12, 2002

I am in New York. I came back for a book-signing session at a bookstore in Queens. I am accompanied by my daughter, Natatsha.

On the day of the signing, my daughter and my cousin Dedzye joined me. It was a very pleasant afternoon. The session ran from noon until 1:30 p.m. We were satisfied with the sales. In addition, we promoted the book in French on the radio and on a television program. I also handed copies of the book to a few journalists in preparation for future interviews. We returned to Montreal convinced that we had done very well. We were pleased with our stay.

As for Jacques, he went back to Haiti for two weeks. He urgently needed to sort out his affairs. He will probably return to Montreal at the end of June.

Part Three

Renovations in the Apartment

Before Jacques left, he had started renovating the basement with Patrick's help. They had begun with the bathroom. Patrick's father replaced my husband for the rest of the work. There were modifications to be made to the electrical system so that each tenant could have their own meter. It was a lot of work. And a very uncomfortable situation for me, since I usually slept in the basement. I mentioned this in my journal.

June 16, 2002

It is 3:30 in the morning. I can't fall asleep. I've been awake since 1:30 a.m. My head is filled with all kinds of thoughts. I don't know what is causing all this turmoil.

For a month now, I haven't been sleeping in my bed. I left my room. With the basement under renovation, I've been sleeping in Elle-Camay's room or at my sister Irène's house. Patrick had planned two weeks of renovation. It has now been a month. I feel like I can't take it anymore. I'm going to crack. I pray to God to calm me down. I long to sleep in my bed again and return to my own things. I've fallen behind. Since Irène also fell ill, I looked after her during the first two weeks of June. Now I yearn for a bit of peace and privacy.

What makes the situation worse is that Jacques continues his childish fits of jealousy. Before leaving for Haiti, he wrote to my editor telling him not to work for me anymore, which I did not take at all well. He photocopied two pages from my personal journal and sent them to my editor. He also made a scene about the mysterious lover in my book. I just cannot understand his behavior.

Having had enough of his infantile reactions, I no longer want to live with him as my husband. I believe I have the right to take a little vacation, to see more clearly within myself. As for my book, I regret nothing I wrote. After all, it is my life I am talking about. I attacked no one. I can't wait to start the second volume.

If I continue to live in the basement with Natatsha and my grandchildren, it is because I currently don't have the strength to rent an apartment far from my family. It would be too painful for me.

The New Place

Natasha's New Hair Salon

In the meantime, Patrick finished the renovation work. I was able to resume my activities, and Jacques returned from Haiti. He had lost even more weight. It seems that every time he comes back from Haiti, he is thinner, weaker, and exhausted. We tease him about it, and he laughs.

July 1, 2002

Today, Monday, I am at Natasha's new salon on Sauvé Street, near Rue de la Jeunesse. It is 1:30 p.m. I am alone here. Jacques and Natasha have gone out to pick up hydraulic chairs. For the past four days, we have been working to renovate the place so that we can begin operations on Tuesday, July 2.

July 12, 2002

I have not been able to write for two weeks. I am delighted for Natasha, who is realizing one of her greatest dreams: to be the sole owner of her salon. It is thanks to the good Lord that all this was made possible. She gave everything she had to make it happen. Since she no longer got along with her associate at the Laurier Street salon, she had to consult a lawyer and was forced to withdraw from the partnership to settle the dispute. Fortunately, all that is now behind her.

Natasha is doing excellent work in her new salon. She designed a beautiful décor. Her father helped her a little, especially with the electrical installation. I also contributed in various ways. Clients love this elegant salon. They feel more comfortable there. I myself enjoy being there; I spend almost every day there, even when I am not working. It is also true that I stay away from home because of the renovations.

On Saturday, July 7, my friend Anièce's daughter, whom I have known since childhood, got married. I rejoiced in their happiness. It was a beautiful wedding. Natasha, Patrick, and Jacques also attended. The rest of the day was very pleasant. During the evening, Jacques was very affectionate. As for me, I tried to be loving with him as before, but I could not. I no longer feel anything for him. I was forced to pretend.

That night, I was compelled to make an effort to be intimate with him. The cause of my rejection is certainly the memory of all the harm he has done to me. He shut the door on the little love I still had for him. I will never forget that he sent my editor photocopies of two pages from my private journal. The height of stupidity and childishness. That violation of my inner world hurt me deeply, because I never wanted my editor (or Jacques, for that matter) to read those words. To make it worse, a letter full of crude remarks accompanied the photocopies. No, I will never forgive him for that shameful and repugnant act.

After his return from Haiti, I did not make love to him for almost a month. To discourage him from touching me, I went to bed every night keeping my underwear on. All of this causes me so much pain. I no longer know what the best solution would be. If it were not for my book, I would leave and go somewhere all alone. I am at the end of my rope.

Chapter 16

The Hair Salon, Beautiful Encounters

Part One

The hair salon was the scene of many events. And if we came to settle in the neighborhood, it was certainly the divine spirit that led us there, my daughter and me. It was in the salon that I met my good friend Renata with whom I had many adventures, and we still do. She lived in the neighborhood. It was summer then, and I would see her pass by every day in the street. She always wore a white blouse.

I felt drawn to Renata. I didn't speak of it to anyone. One fine day, Natatsha and I were in the salon, she came in saying: "Hi, I'm Renata, I live next door. I'm a writer, I write fiction stories." We responded to her greeting. Natatsha introduced herself as the owner of the salon, then introduced me in these terms: "Here's my mother, she's always here with me." And she went on: "She too is a writer; she has just written the first volume of her autobiography." Opening her eyes with a beautiful smile, Renata said to me: "My respects, madam, I congratulate you." I thanked her. After a few minutes of conversation, she left, expressing a brief greeting from the house. Since then, she came to see us almost every day. But she did not linger. At some point, I felt the need to offer her a copy of my book.

One morning, she stayed a little longer chatting with us. I invited her to follow me into the office located at the back of the salon. I offered her the book while slipping in these words: "I felt that I had to do it." She thanked me with tears in her eyes. Moved myself; I was on the verge of tears. She gave me a big hug. She asked me questions about distribution and my new writing projects. I told her that we were looking for a translator, etc. She left very touched. Toward the end of the afternoon, she came back. Here is what I wrote a little later in my journal.

Journal

I had finished my workday when Renata returned to the salon to tell us that she would feel honored to translate my book; she wished, in doing so, to be able to rediscover memories she had buried deep in her heart. She planned to read the work at the same time as she translated it. She even brought us the beginning of the translation. During our conversation, we realized that we had many things in common.

And so, this is how we found our translator for the book. Afterwards, we undertook several other activities together. Sometimes, she would bring us good soup, her personal vegetarian recipe. We have remained very good friends.

Part Two

Touching Reunions

One day, I was at the salon with Natatsha and Jacques, who had come to fix something for my daughter. My cell phone rang; it was my friend (the mysterious lover) calling me: "I'm in Montreal," he announced. "I just spoke to your sister; she gave me your number. She invited me to dinner, but she told me that you should tell me which day suits you best." I immediately replied: "Tomorrow at 5 PM, I'll be at her place." He confirmed that he would be there.

The next day, I informed Jacques that my sister was inviting me to dinner because she had a friend arriving from New York. She was counting on me to take him back to his hotel after dinner. I told him that I would then need my car. Since he had returned to Montreal, he had been using my car to go do his renovation work.

So, I attended the dinner. It had been at least 20 years since I had last seen my friend. I was delighted to see him again. I told him about myself, my activities, and my book. I dedicated a copy to him. He, in turn, spoke about himself, his work, and what had changed in his life, etc. At the end of the evening, I took him back to his hotel. Our meeting had been extremely pleasant. Upon his return to New York, he called me, but I couldn't speak because Jacques was nearby. He had given me his business card, and I wrote to him. He had now simply become a friend. He has a wife and children. It feels good to see again someone you once loved.

Part Three

Jacques' Tricks

I couldn't guess Jacques' real intentions. He tried to be very kind to me. He hadn't let go of his subtle surveillance methods. He spied on everything I did. He even checked if I was hiding things under my pillows. He constantly monitored my phone calls. But he did it in a barely perceptible way. One day, he accompanied me to a work meeting. There was a round table, and I was one of the guests. I had entrusted him with my books and my suitcase. While I was on the stage, I noticed him rummaging through my suitcase, looking for I don't know what. I became very nervous. I had difficulty concentrating; it was terrible. All the while, he appeared gentle and calm.

This man did even worse. He had opened a small printing business in the room at the back of the salon. One day, he was absent all afternoon. I assumed he had gone to carry out some renovation work. Leaving the salon at the end of the day, I went straight home. I immediately turned on my computer to check my email. Since the server wasn't responding, I checked if the device was plugged in. To my great astonishment, I noticed that several wires had been connected. The telephone wire, in particular, led to a locked briefcase. At that moment, I realized: Jacques had bugged me, just as he had done in our house on Boyer Street! In fact, this incident had precipitated our first separation in 1995. I was completely shocked! I immediately disconnected the wire and reconnected the computer. It started working right away. I then called Natatsha and told her everything. The incident plunged me into a state of extreme nervousness. I no longer knew how to act.

When Jacques returned, I remained silent about my discovery.

He, of course, believed that I was still being monitored. He laughed at everything and nothing and rambled almost nonstop with coarse nonsense. On my side, I restrained myself from shouting my disgust. On top of all that, he had hijacked my phone account and was constantly dialing the number of an anonymous client in New York State. As a result, I ended up with an exorbitant bill. But I continued to remain silent. In fact, I was waiting for the right moment to expose all his wrongdoing with impact. He wanted war at all costs he would get it.

As a precaution, I entrusted all my important documents to my daughter. She reiterated her warning: "Mammy, avoid provoking him. With him, you must, for now, use diplomacy. And don't change any of your habits. But still make an appointment as soon as possible with your lawyer and explain what happened. Don't talk to anyone else, including your beloved sister."

While going through these painful moments, I remained sensitive to my environment and to what was happening in the world. This is reflected in the following passage from my journal.

Journal

Memory of September 11, 2001

It is the anniversary of the September 11, 2001 attack in Manhattan, New York State. I don't know why, but I don't feel well. Deep down, there is sadness. I think of the people who lost their lives, those who survived, the families who lost a loved one, and also the spectators like us.

Despite everything, there is still a positive effect to be drawn from this event. Today, people take the time to look around them. To finally see that other humans share this space. That they are not alone on this planet. They take the time to live better, realizing that there is a force guiding us in our daily activities.

I think of my little nephew Maki who lives in Manhattan. On the day of the event, I called him to ask how he was. He replied in a sad voice: "Aunt Enice, did you see that we have lost our New York?" Since that day, I felt that something was not right in him. I know other people, and I have friends who were deeply affected by this event. I pray for them and believe that humanity should change the way it lives.

Montreal Book Fair

It is 3 a.m. It's the day of the Montreal Book Fair. I have been awake since 2 a.m. and cannot go back to sleep. I have just realized the magnitude of the event I am going to participate in, and that it will be magnificent for me. I thank God for it. He loves me greatly, and I love Him too.

I participated in the Book Fair on Thursday, November 14, 2002.

For me, it was a success in every way. My health allowing, I held up until the end. Socially, it was wonderful: the public showed me sympathy. In terms of sales, it was fabulous. Regarding my children and friends, there were many affectionate gestures. Everything is fine, and I am proud of myself. I thank Natatsha, who supported me morally.

My daughter, despite her work, gave me constant assistance and greatly encouraged me. My sister Irène also supported me, as did my son, even though he could not attend the Fair. The writer Dany Laferrière guided me very discreetly. I felt uplifted by the generous support of all these people.

I can only rejoice in everything happening to me. At the Fair, I received news from a friend who, like me, had once been a boarder with the nuns. I had lost touch with her for more than 30 years. Having noticed my book in a bookstore, she bought it. Since she could not attend the Fair, she asked her daughter to bring it to me for a dedication. At the same time, she sent written comments that deeply moved me. I also want to mention a lady accompanied by her daughter, who bought four copies of the book. She planned to send them to friends living abroad.

The reception my book received far exceeded my expectations. It was truly wonderful. People who had heard me in radio or television interviews came, despite the bad weather, to meet me. Oh, Jesus, how beautiful is what You have done for me! And I must not forget to mention the presence, all day long, of my very dear friend Renata. Constantly by my side, she took care of me like my good angel. I will never thank her enough.

There you have it! This is the unforgettable memory I keep of my participation in the Montreal Book Fair.

Part Four

Hospitalization of Elle-Camay / Journal

December 7, 2002

It is noon. I am at Sainte-Justine Hospital in the room where Elle-Camay has been hospitalized since 10 a.m. I have come to replace Natatsha. Elle-Camay is suffering from a throat infection and has swollen glands. She is in a lot of pain. She turned seven on December 3. She celebrated her birthday in the hospital. She received many gifts from the hospital staff and from family.

Elle-Camay stayed nine days in the hospital. Things went fairly well, because each time she went to receive her treatments, which were rather painful, the doctor would give her a stuffed animal.

The intense exposure to fatigue was mostly for Natatsha and me. Natatsha stayed with her daughter at night, and I went during the day. While caring for Elle-Camay, I thought of my son, who had to take exams for a position with the City of Montreal. I prayed for him. He got the job. So everything was going well for the family. We ended the year beautifully and were very happy. Before the end-of-year holidays, I participated in several book signing sessions at bookstores and other venues where I was invited.

Chapter 17

A Breakup Letter

The Beginning of 2003

Part One

We spent New Year's Day quietly with the family, as usual. After the exhaustion I had just experienced, I deserved a few days of rest. I would then be ready to start the year off on the right foot. January was peaceful. But Jacques was still spying on me. My heart was heavy.

Before the holidays, I had called my lawyer to schedule an appointment. Despite everything, I had not yet decided which course of action to take. I continued to reflect on the whole matter. This time, I was determined not to go back. Consequently, things had to be done properly and complete discretion maintained. February was coming to an end.

I reproduce here a passage from my journal.

February 26, 2003

I haven't written since the beginning of the year, and yet I have a lot to share. These days, I find it difficult to concentrate, especially when I feel that I am being spied on.

February 28, 2003

I am at the Saint-Hubert restaurant in Montreal-Nord. I am alone and feel well. I ordered a meal and then a fruit cocktail. I am waiting for the time to go to a meeting organized by an association dedicated to the Creole language. The meeting place is not far from the restaurant. I am taking my time. I don't have my car. Jacques damaged it to the point that I will have to buy another one. He came to drop me off at the restaurant very early. To pass the time, I visit a small shopping center. Natatsha has agreed to pick me up after her work. I am not worried.

Between Jacques and me, day by day, the situation worsens.

We argue constantly, to the point that Mikaël, Natatsha's 4-year-old boy, gets angry at Jacques: "Why do you yell so loudly at Grandma? She isn't mean, you make her cry all the time!" Jacques amuses himself by writing me letters, sometimes saying silly things, sometimes reproaching me. He does not leave me alone for a second. I cannot see any other man, and anyway, I am not thinking about that. I already have one who is too much for me, why look elsewhere! Moreover, I no longer trust men. I am at my breaking point.

Although I take sleeping pills, I do not sleep well. I live with constant stress. My heart races at the slightest noise. It has created a vulnerability in me that makes me anxious, distressed, and drained like a zombie. I am really sick. My appointment with my lawyer is scheduled for the end of March.

I am going to meet the lawyer, and my daughter accompanies me. I inform him of everything: "Madame Toussaint," he asks me, "is this time serious? And are you ready for the divorce?" My answer is prompt and firm: "Yes, Maître, and as quickly as possible. This time, I am not leaving; he must leave. For that, I must personally hand him the document initiating the divorce proceedings." He shows curiosity about how I am going to proceed. I explain to him that since Jacques must leave for Haiti on April 15, I will give him the document upon his return to Montreal, on the evening of May 17, 2003. He will have to leave the house immediately. The lawyer and my daughter advise me to grant him a one-day grace period, and I accept their advice. The lawyer concludes the meeting with this encouraging remark:

"This is the first time I see you confident; I trust you. I now have all the relevant information. I will call you in May to come pick up the legal document."

He shakes our hands, and we take our leave.

March 21, 2003

This morning, I stayed in bed. I am in too much pain all over. I prayed to God to enlighten me and to heal me from all the illnesses that dominate my body, and to help me understand myself better. I know I have a mission on earth, and I would like to accomplish it, but for that, I need all my health and the unwavering support of an angel.

I long for calm and to take care of only myself.

Now, I am seeking peace. I have been awake since 4 a.m. Since I cannot fall back asleep, I decided to get up. I wrote a little. I am thinking about the spring that has finally arrived. I will feel good, as it is my favorite season. Just thinking about it makes me feel alive. And I just remembered to check the winning lottery numbers.

I checked online and saw that I had 5 correct numbers out of 6 in Quebec 49, which meant I had won $500. I was happy. I thanked God for this beautiful gift He had given me.

April 3, 2003

Patrick had invited me along with his mother to the Saint-Denis Theatre to attend the performance by the group "Shoboulou d'Haïti." Luck Merville was also supposed to perform. We went to the show that evening. It was nice; Luck gave a very good performance. I liked him a lot. The next day, I was so tired. I couldn't stand to hear anyone. There had been too much noise in the theater.

I continue my story

Jacques was supposed to leave for Haiti on April 15, 2003. As for me, I planned to go to Quebec to attend the Book Fair on April 14, 2003. He offered to take me to Quebec that day. I accepted. During the trip, our exchanges were rather brief. I was searching for my words. The atmosphere was heavy. This man, who was my husband, had played so many cruel tricks on me that I no longer trusted him and could no longer find anything to say to him. I resisted the temptation to hate him, but I disapproved of what he had done to me: "You shall not hate your neighbor." So commands the divine commandment.

Journal, April 14, 2003

I have decided to write about what has been happening to me over the past few days.

To begin, on April 12, I went to the Quebec Book Fair. I enjoyed the experience. People appreciated my book a lot, and I sold some as well. By the end of the day, I was exhausted, especially since I had to return to Montreal that same evening.

On Thursday evening, I had an argument with Jacques regarding my response to a letter he had written me. Two weeks ago, as I have already mentioned, he had put me under surveillance.

He had done this before, and this disgraceful act had caused our first separation in June 1995. This must also be added to all the acts of malice I endured during the 28 years I spent with him. I had a premonition that if I did not act, we would one day end up killing each other. I had decided to write him a breakup letter before his departure for Haiti, and another letter attached to a birthday card on the day of his departure.

Breakup Letter

Sunday, April 13, 2003

I would like you to take the time to read my letter carefully.

My dear Jacques,

I have realized that we can no longer communicate as we once did about our feelings; there is a barrier. On my side, I have changed a lot. As for my feelings toward you, I do not know! You know, when I do something, it is because there is a reason. Regarding the accusations you made against me, claiming that I slept with another man, I find it disrespectful because, since I have been with you (1973), I have never betrayed you, and I am proud of that because I kept the promise I made to you, while you broke yours. The love I had for you has turned into pity, and I have realized that this is the reason we could no longer communicate. This barrier remains and is not going away.

I thought I could remove it, but it is too heavy for me. I have understood that if I do not let go, I will lose myself, and we will end up hating each other. I want to avoid that at all costs. It is better for us to part ways while remaining friends. For now, we are roommates. Upon your return from Haiti, you will look for a place to live by June. If you need any help and I am not busy, I will be there for you. I have thought a lot about our situation, and I believe this is the best decision for both of us.

You think I am calling New York to contact a lover. No, Jacques, you are mistaken. I do not want a man in my life right now. I have so many things to do. You should realize that romantic adventures do not interest me at the moment. I need to start my second book; for that, I need time for myself. This is very serious for me; it is not a game. Moreover, because of all I have endured over these years, I need to breathe and enjoy my freedom.

Do not forget that we have our children and grandchildren, whom we love dearly and who love us. Do not worry; I will explain the situation to them with love. They will understand, and since you will always be welcome, it will not be like previous times.

I must leave now, my dear friend, otherwise I will be late for church. Before your departure, I will write you another letter. No hard feelings!

With friendship,
Enice T.

I continue my story

I gave Jacques the second letter on the morning of his departure, before he took the plane. I had placed it inside a card for his birthday, which was on April 19.

During his absence, I prepared the divorce petition with my lawyer. I also prepared myself mentally for his return. I rearranged the apartment, removing all his personal belongings and storing them in a room in the basement. For business reasons, I then went on a trip, accompanied by my daughter.

Monday, April 14, 2003

Dear friend,

Do you remember when you brought the little dog Toby home? At that time, the children were young, and we were overjoyed to welcome him into the family. He was cute and innocent. It was wonderful. You were the Jacques I knew before. We were a happy family, and for me, it was for life.

It is true that things were not always perfect. You know, people change and grow older! It is like little Toby, who grew up to be big and strong but still remained loyal to his owners. You, however, began to change gradually, and even more so after your mother's death. And it worsened day by day. The children also changed, as did

I, in fact. Time itself changes things; that is life, and we should follow its course. We should then follow our destiny, and do so without hating each other as so many others do. Now, Jacques, you understand what I want to tell you through this letter.

With that, I leave you. I wish you a happy birthday and a joyful Easter. Take care of yourself in Haiti.

With all friendship,
Enice

Trip to New York with my sister by bus

May 5, 2003

I woke up this morning in New York. I am at Aunt Dadia's with my sister Irène. It is 6:30 a.m., and the weather is nice. The sun has begun to rise. My sister, who shares the bed with me, has not yet gotten up. Aunt Dadia and her daughter are still sleeping in another room. I feel good. I feel alive; I am elated. There is something within me that makes me want to move. "Energy, what else." I want to write, to share this happiness with others through writing.

I have been in New York since Friday morning with Irène. This is the first time I have traveled with her, and this occasion will allow me to get to know her a little better. We had a good trip. We arrived at the Port Authority terminal in Manhattan and transferred to a bus for Queens.

Aunt Dadia came to pick us up at the station. I was tired because we had traveled all night. I felt weak. I had not slept much during the trip. And given my physical state, because of my exhaustion, I was a bit nervous and avoided talking as much as possible.

Chapter 18

Jacques' Return to Montreal

My Separation and Divorce

Jacques returned to Montreal on May 17, 2003. During his stay in Haiti, he had been harassing me with emails full of lies and absurd accusations. At some point, I stopped reading them. When he called, it was to monitor my every move and to shout nonsense at me. Over time, I became afraid to speak to him. I no longer answered his questions, since I already knew what I had to do.

No one was aware of my plan except my daughter.

During my stay in New York with my sister and my aunt, Natatsha and I had discreetly informed a few close friends that I was going to file for divorce. They did not believe me. They expressed doubts: "Are you sure, Nounoune, that you're going to do it?" Their reaction annoyed me a little: "That's why I didn't want to tell you." I continued: "I am very serious and determined. I told you. Let's not talk about it anymore! Let's move on to other things."

I went to pick him up at the airport. As usual, he had lost weight. I gave him a light kiss on the lips. On the way home, we exchanged news about family members in Montreal and Haiti. Before his arrival, I had carefully packed his personal belongings and stored them in a room in the basement. Everything was ready for the execution of my plan. I had also collected the relevant documents from my lawyer's office.

Upon arriving home, we went straight up to Natatsha's, who had prepared dinner for the whole family. After greetings and finishing dinner, we went downstairs. He did not hide his surprise: "What's going on? The room looks bigger." I replied, "I did some major cleaning." He sat at my computer and tried to access my email.

He seemed annoyed: "Did you change your password?" My response was evasive: "A lot of things have changed." I opened a drawer in my desk, took out the document, and told him, "You know, Jacques, it has been a long time since there was any life between us. The relationship between us has become too negative. Before hatred sets in, I think it's better for us to separate." He replied, "It's your decision."

I presented him with the document and gave this warning: "Here is the divorce petition. You have until tomorrow to leave." Silently, he took the document and opened it to read. Suddenly feeling pity, I made him this offer: "If you haven't found a place yet, I will give you until Sunday." It was Friday evening. He timidly said, "Yes."

I quickly changed the subject. I could sense he was nervous. I set this condition: "You cannot sleep next to me in the bed." I went to bed. He could not sleep, and the light did not help. I said to him, "It's late, I need to sleep." He went to the bathroom. Then he came to speak to me: "I'm too tired; I can't sleep on the mattress on the floor. For one night, can I sleep next to you?" I agreed.

As soon as he lay down in the bed, he tried to restrain me. He whispered, "We will make love one last time." I forcefully freed myself and replied, "You know, we made love for the last time on April 15, 2003, the day before you left for Haiti. So, my dear, I will never make love with you again. Saying it's the last time only leads to more times, and it's over." I added, "If you try to touch me, I will scream, and the children will rush in to see what is happening."

He remained lying in bed, turned his back, and fell asleep. Trembling with fear, I feared he might try to touch me again.

The next day, he left around noon. He went to his cousin's to ask if he could stay there. That day, I did not leave the house. In the late evening, I prepared a good dinner. After his departure, I sat in a chair and thought: "This is the first time I refused to give Jacques sex and resisted him. I am proud of myself. Thank you, Jesus."

I truly felt strong. I had no feelings of sadness or hatred toward Jacques. I had found serenity. Upon his return, he ate. Then he told me that his cousin agreed to set up a room for him at her place, and he would leave the next day. He did not need to worry about anything, as I had already packed all his belongings into boxes. The next day, he calmly loaded everything onto a trailer. By noon, he was finished.

Before leaving, he came to say goodbye. He hugged me while murmuring, "Enice, you know, this is the first time in my life that I am afraid." I replied, "You know, Jacques, this is the first time since I have been with you that I feel this strong. You have always taken all my strength. I have always been afraid, but now I feel good. I am no longer afraid, and I feel strong."

I wished him, "Good luck." He kissed me again and left. For a few seconds, I felt a sense of compassion for him. But immediately, I regained myself. I went out to see him to his vehicle. I watched him drive away. Back in my room, I said aloud, "I never want to be the slave of any man again." This is my deep commitment. Thank you, Jesus!

Today, May 19, 2003,

It is 4:30 a.m. I have just finished my last manuscript. Thank you, Jesus!

Author's Reflection

While writing the first volume of the book" Tale of a Multifaceted Life",

I experienced a feeling of well-being. I felt framed by the warm affection that my parents brought me, the union and love that reigned in the family, and the generosity of both my parents towards their neighbor, which also moved me. Until the inevitable happened, which turned my life upside down. It was the best part of my life.

At my young age, my mother died. My resentment at my separation between my sister Irene and my brother Robert was a second heartbreak. I remember a strong sister, a protector with the rigor of war.

A father defines himself as a hero in the eyes of his daughter, but mine described himself as disloyal. The love I had for my father was stronger than hatred. So, I recognized his helplessness, which is why I forgave him.

Throughout my childhood and adolescence, I felt the power of ignorance and the carefree nature of the human being.
Relentless changes. Ignorance was still there in another form. New environment, new social class, new friends. Despite all this, in my heart, there was love. My shyness in love.

The desire to die is to join my mother. The revelation that saved me from this hell and took me to Sister Berthe, whose instinct makes me feel that I have found safety.

Then, I found myself in an unwanted marriage that I could never accept. My naivety, and my fear. This man's infidelity, disrespect, and wickedness prevented me from opening my heart to him.

Until my second marriage to Jacques, which was celebrated in turmoil. Little did I think at the time that this freely accepted and desired choice would lead me down such a torturous path that it could only be imagined by the greatest of prophets. Was there a
particle of happiness in this dream life? The hope of a finally stabilized life as a couple

was on the horizon, I told myself! In my mind, everything was in place to allow us to give our children every possible chance of success, so that one day, we would contemplate with joy and pride their happiness through us and with us.

But they did ' t count on the other party, who made up the couple. Without realizing it, or out of disbelief, I found myself, without warning, on a downward slope from all points of view: social, family, material, economic, etc. All these unfortunate episodes are related to you in these books that I had a lot of difficulty in undertaking writing.

Today, you are going to share with me all the adventures I have had to face, to end up learning to revolt a little bit from these situations of baseness, submission, and even sexual slavery, suddenly at the hands of a being who behaved with us like an inhuman, soulless concentration camp leader, of no civility, barbarous, and retrograde.

I am exposing to you in these lines an important part of my intimacy that has deeply humiliated me. Because I am aware today that all this should not have lasted so long.

Thus, we often hear this reflection: Life is a long, quiet river that flows peacefully at sea. In my case, it seems that mine flowed in the opposite direction, which corresponded
to the tormented life I had with my two ex-spouses. So, I had no hope of getting through all the torments, tribulations, injustices, disappointments, and taunts of all kinds at the hands of a man who wanted to remain my husband at all costs, but on his terms.

Fortunately, I have found in writing the necessary strength to free myself from its clutches and share with you all these ridiculous " comings and goings & quot; that have shaped my life, that I presented to you in the form of confessions, and confessions in my first books.

In " A Woman Among Many Others, volumes 1, 2, and 3, I applied myself to telling the story of my torturous life under the control of a sadist whom I took too long to identify as such. I came out alive and proud to be able to present you this fourth and last Volume,

& quot; Tale of a Multifaceted Life, to close this chapter of my life surrounded by my family.

On that note, enjoy reading, and I ask you not to judge me too harshly, because I am aware today that all this should not have lasted so long.

Thank you.

Author: Enice Toussaint

A Woman Among Many Writes, by Enice Toussaint, is the fourth volume in a series of four volumes, published by

Édition Nouveau Siècle
ENS Publishing

For information, contact Natasha Casimir

Visit our website: www.enspublishing.com
Email: ediontionsens@gmail.com

Éditions Nouveau Siècle

www.ingramcontent.com/pod-product-compliance
Lightning Source LLC
Chambersburg PA
CBHW061230070526
44584CB00030B/4059